KNITTING
FOR
REAL PEOPLE

Ferne Geller Cone

Photographs by J. Morton Cone and Joe Coca
Drawings by Susan Lee Azadi and Ann Sabin
Cartoon by Phil Garland
Cover design by Signorella Graphic Arts
"What Is a Sweater?" provided by Ardyce Uhrich

Some yarns contributed by Lisle Yarns and Cosmos Rabbit Factory
Information on wool provided by The Wool Bureau, Inc.

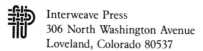

Interweave Press
306 North Washington Avenue
Loveland, Colorado 80537

ISBN 0-934026-47-5
Library of Congress Catalog Number 89-11135
First printing: 7.5M:1189:OB

Library of Congress Cataloging-in-Publication Data
Cone, Ferne Geller.
    Knitting for real people.
    1. Knitting   I. Title.
TT820.C7837   1989   746.9'2—dc20   89-11135

To my friend, Gladys Nelson

Acknowledgments

A single phrase triggered the idea for this book—
"Can I?" To all knitters who have ever uttered those
words, many thanks.

Special appreciation must be given to my editor
Linda Ligon, who patiently, with encouragement and
humor, chauffeured me from conception to finished
manuscript; to my dear friends Joyce Arizumi and
Jerri Chaplin, professionals in other fields, who so
graciously posed for several photos; to the other
models—the three delightful Schimanski sisters, Kay,
Lee, and Jo; to Sandy Naon, Juanita Kennedy,
Cynthia Tsark, and to my precious and precocious
granddaughter, Stephanie Dore, my grateful thanks.

Thank you to the people at Tinctoria who allowed
me to use their classroom for a whole year; and to my
talented artist, Susan Lee Azadi, who painstakingly
interpreted details and who also modeled. Special
appreciation to Dr. Carol Anne Dickson, Professor of
Fashion Merchandising at the University of Hawaii,
who believes in my theories; and to Orpha Herrick,
former head of the Department of Textile and Clothing at the University of Hawaii, for her tips on proportion. To J. Morton Cone for his ever-ready camera
and always available shoulder, love.

When presenting new, and perhaps "offbeat," ideas
one must be able to bounce them off experienced as
well as less experienced listeners; my deepest gratitude
for allowing me to share their thoughts and concerns
to THE GROUP:

Jo Baskerville
Mary Biele
Jackie Leake
Muriel Lightfoot
Beverly Merrihew
Barbara Richardson
Carol Schimanski
Lee Schimanski
Eleanor Thienes
Joan Harshman (honorary)

TABLE OF CONTENTS

What is a Sweater?

A sweater is a state of mind, A moment of truth, a promise.

A sweater is an extension of the woman who wears it, The appreciation of the man who sees her in it, The creative expression of the one who made it.

For the one who wears it, it is a status symbol, A social commentary, an emotional facade, a self revelation. A pride of individuality. A proof of taste. A yearning.

For the ones who see us in it, A sweater is an embellishment. A pit fall. An ambush. A subtlety. Mirage. Camouflage. Persiflage. An intoxication.

For those who make them, A sweater is an evolution, a sign of the times. A symphony of lines, a harmony of tones, A tribute to skills. A drip-dry. Hip-tie. Zip-shy masterpiece.

A sweater is an art-and-a-craft. A pull-on. A slip-on. A cardigan. A shirt.

A one-piece. Two-piece. Three piece. A no-peace. It is a vision, a trend, an interpretation. A guess. A hope. A prayer. A sketch. A swatch. A sample. It is 2 or 200 needles and 12,345 stitches.

It is the livable, breathable, wearable offspring of The shearer, the carder, the spinner, the dyer, the knitter, The designer, the pattern-maker, the button-baker, the order-taker.

It is snips of yarn. Sips of coffee.

It is a bid for immortality. It is the star to which hitch The dreams and schemes of the fashion writers, advertisers, buyers, merchandisers, and ultimately, The one who wears it.

—Ardyce Uhrich

INTRODUCTION

As consumers, we sometimes behave like puppets on a string. Someone tells us what to wear, what to eat, what kind of car to drive, what's hot, and what's not. Much of the time we're not even aware that these decisions are being made for us. Did you know that a panel of professional colorists decides what colors we'll be wearing a couple of years ahead of time? Designers pay attention to these pronouncements, and these "hot" colors turn up in their collections on cue. And we follow along like a bunch of sheep.

But sometimes we need to be jolted out of this pattern. We need to be adventurous and try something because it suits us. We can choose colors and designs that "make our day," not those of the designers who profit from dictating change, change, change.

One area of fashion that for years has dangled its devotees on puppet strings is handknitting. Not by dictating ever-constant change, but the reverse—by allowing little change. The puppet strings are labeled *always* and *never*: always knit skirts on circular needles; never wear knitted skirts if you're heavy; always follow a pattern when you knit; never mix certain colors. Thinking in such absolute terms produces copycat knitters who blindly follow someone else's dictates. I hope this book will help change that. It's about learning some simple basics and taking off on your own—adapting knitting to your own special needs.

At the conclusion of a recent workshop, one of my students heaved a big sigh and expressed appreciation for finally discovering that even someone with her generous measurements could successfully create, knit, and wear a handknit that fit beautifully and was fashionable as well. In that same workshop, another student, who weighed about 95 pounds, was equally delighted because, she, too, found that she could produce a well-designed garment to suit her petite figure.

"Knits make me look like a sausage tied in the middle." "I'm too skinny." "Only skinnies can wear handknits." "I'm too fat." "I'm never sure about color." "Knits are too clingy." "I've always knitted from a pattern book." "Someone has to write out the directions for me." "Patterns are never small enough for me and I have to use little kids' designs, but they always look just like what they are—kids' clothes." These are direct quotes, and I constantly hear variations of them. They are all valid comments, but I have learned from experience that all of these so-called problems can have successful solutions.

1

Knitting *is* for real people

Why do we knit? Because it's something to do with our hands while we watch TV; because we're bored at meetings; because we think it's economical; because it's a sensory experience; because it's relaxing. Large percentages of us are on a diet of one kind or another much of the time—and knitting can help keep our hands out of the cookie jar. Many knit because it's chic, and designer sweaters are hot fashion. People with emotional problems or just plain everyday stress knit for therapy. Those recovering from illness have discovered knitting. I speak with authority—knitting saved my sanity while I was recuperating from a spinal fusion. But whatever your reason for knitting, it should also be fun; you should enjoy the process as well as the result. It can be a passport to a whole new world of creativity!

Contrary to public opinion, there is no mystery to this enduring and productive craft. The basic requirements are simple tools and patience while the hands become accustomed to wiggling the yarn around the needles. "But," you say, "I have eleven thumbs and I'm timid about fashion. And all those complicated directions make me crazy." All misconceptions. Desire, tenacity, and a willingness to experiment are all you need for success.

Be fashionable with handknits

Handknits have become one of the most durable fashion statements of our time. Sweater dressing is definitely "in" and knits are no longer shoved to the back of the closet. People who never before wanted to learn to knit are anxious to take needles in hand—from kids in elementary school to fashion-conscious adults, both male and female. Busy career women have discovered the comfort and style of knits, and the soft sweater is replacing the more rigid tailored jacket. With the availability of lighter weight yarns in an astonishing spectrum of colors and textures, knits are for all seasons, and for every *body*.

In this fast-moving, technologically-advancing world, we want and need clothes that won't restrict our body movements and that have fewer closures. Who has time for balky zippers or buttons in hard-to-reach places when they're unnecessary except as decoration? And we're finally paying attention to the needs of the physically handicapped, making it easier for them to dress themselves. No other material can match the flexibility of knitted fabrics.

My travels have taken me to many countries, where I like to observe how people move in their clothes. When I visited Japan, knits were everywhere. The Japanese designers seemed to incorporate that sense of freedom and generosity in their knits which originated with the kimono look—dropped shoulders, roomy sleeves, and fluid materials. In southern Spain as well, where the weather hovers at 75 to 80 degrees year round, sweaters were on everyone, knitted from every type of fiber—including leather.

Manufacturers of handknitting yarns have responded to this heightened awareness and interest, and they are producing delectable fibers in combinations formerly undreamed of. Who would have thought of knitting with mink, or leather, or even strips of woven material? There's something for everybody these days, in all price ranges—a virtual bonanza!

The story behind
Knitting for Real People

This book has been in the back of my mind for a long time, just waiting to be hatched. As a proving ground for my ideas, I called together a group of people interested in knitting. They were all different ages, sizes, and shapes, with varying levels of skill. A few were longtime knitters who could work every intricate pattern stitch ever invented. Others were at the intermediate stage and could follow a commercial pattern with no difficulty. A couple were rank beginners. We even had an honorary member of the group who lives in Michigan. The glue that held the group together was a keen interest in learning how to make independent choices and in creating personal designs—that fit.

We met about once a month here in Seattle for over a year. During our meetings, we discussed and exchanged ideas and goals. The air at our meetings was electric. The enthusiasm of the group convinced me that an area of deficiency for many knitters is understanding how to choose or discard, and how to judge what type of design is flattering. The questions and concerns of group members are the basis for the information in this book. What finally surfaced was the search for permission—permission to break away and experiment. There seemed to be a fear of the unknown, but when we all began to share experiences and the crazy mistakes we had made, everyone relaxed. Once group members understood that plenty of options were available if they were willing to risk a setback or two, they flew like birds. Many of their original designs, along with comments about how they were created, appear throughout this book. Take advantage of their experiences.

One of the goals of the group was to learn to knit skirts. Most had never knitted one—or even considered it. At the end of the year, each had either knitted a skirt or had a design in the works. One person in the group made three tops to go with one skirt! Not everyone will necessarily want to knit a skirt to match a top, but ever since knitting a skirt in elementary school, I've been hooked on the ensemble concept. It makes good sense to think about coordinates, so whenever a new design is in the works, a skirt to match becomes part of my total plan. A knitted skirt can be a time-saver, too, relieving the frustration of racing all over town trying to match material to the yarn, or vice versa. Several skirt designs are illustrated throughout the book, with suggestions on how to achieve satisfying results based on your proportions and color plan. Hints are given about mixing and matching with other garments already in your closet.

Set yourself free

There are dozens of books describing knitting dos and don'ts, and thousands of commercial patterns are available, but their rigidity can be somewhat stifling. In my opinion, *appropriateness* shares equal billing with *technique*. Technique is useless if the results aren't attractive and satisfying. With such an abundance of choices, you can feel free to take features from several sources to make up your own combination for a special garment. Based on the information in this book, you should be able to create a signature knit that fits—one that you will design from simple shapes without complicated mathematics. And more important, you'll be proud to take credit for it from the first loop on the needle to the very last stitch.

Proportion in design is as important in knitted clothing as it is in clothing made from woven fabric, and I think easier to achieve. Together with proportion, color, texture, and shape play crucial roles. We'll discuss some of the critical things to keep an eye out for when creating with yarn, so that the end result has a professional quality that will make you look good and well-turned-out.

Knitters cringe at the idea of ripping out precious stitches. In their minds, ripping is associated with failure. Malarky! As I emphasize in every book I've written and in every workshop I teach, mistakes happen to all of us, even highly-skilled professionals. Some of the most interesting and enduring designs were the direct result of mistakes. What I've learned from each of my mistakes is that there are no absolutes. What's more, I still do some goofy things, even now. So if you can accept ripping out as part of the learning process, you will open the door to a new attitude about knitting. And once you learn about gauge, you'll rip very little—but more about that later.

Along with an understanding of how to knit, in my opinion, it is equally important to know how to alter your knits—whether to accommodate figure changes, or to update and/or change what you've already produced. Many professionals may not agree with my approach. As a matter of fact, many are adamant about not reknitting garments; they suggest giving them away or tossing them out. This horrifies me. It's wasteful and uneconomical. We're a throwaway society as it is, so why add to it? I'm suggesting that you re-use previously knitted yarn, provided it is possible to reclaim it in good condition. I have found that careful laundering or steaming will usually revitalize unraveled yarn. So far, no circumstances have been drastic enough to warrant abandoning any of my "babies"—my favorite handknits.

You have several choices when it's time to put all the bits and pieces together. These choices are described, with pros and cons, so that you'll be able to make intelligent decisions. Each is illustrated by drawings of the techniques and photos of finished garments.

A collection of designs is included in the book. The garments described appear on real people, not professional models. Some specifics are given, but not always stitch-by-stitch directions, for that would defeat the purpose of the book. After you've read the book, you should be able to adapt any of the designs to your own measurements and taste—and probably improve on them. I'd love to hear about how you do.

I have tried to describe techniques and tricks in easily understandable language so that you will see how simple it can be to create your own designs from scratch. You will discover how much fun you can have with knitting. I guarantee it!

Chapter 1
NEEDLES, YARN, AND SOME KEY TERMS

To knit, you need only a pair of knitting needles and some yarn. Of course, it also helps to have a little patience and some practice—and an idea of what you're going to knit. But more about that later.

Needles

My hope is that this book will free you from the need to be told what needle size to use, and will encourage you to make that decision for yourself, to suit the particular yarns you've chosen, and the kind of fabric you want to achieve. If you plan to do a lot of knitting, you'd be wise to acquire several sizes and types of needles, to be prepared for any project when the creative urge hits. As you progress as an independent knitter, you might find yourself working on several projects at the same time, using the *same* size needles. This has been my own experience, so my knitting bag holds several pairs of each size. When I'm on a roll, having those extra pairs has been a real time-saver.

Knitting needles can be made from many materials—aluminum, steel, plastic, wood, nylon, bone, and bamboo. Which type you use is a matter of personal preference. I've tried them all, but find that I'm partial to aluminum needles. The points are well-defined and not too sharp, and they don't split the yarn. They never wear out and are available in several colors. You can choose a color to contrast with the yarn, which helps to identify stitches more easily.

Some people swear by plastic needles and won't use anything else. My main objections to plastic needles are that they can easily break or bend, and when used with synthetic yarns, the heat generated by your hands can cause the yarn to stick to the needles. Nylon needles have a tendency to lose their "heads," and the stitches may slip off the end. The points are too sharp for me and I must always be on the alert for split yarn.

I first tested bamboo needles during a trip to Japan many years ago when other types were not available. They filled the bill in an emergency, but I still prefer the aluminum.

Heavy use can cause wooden needles to become rough, and this can damage your yarn. They need to be sanded down and oiled every once in a while, and who wants to fool around with that? Besides, they're heavier than most other types of needles.

Straight needles always come in pairs. They vary in length: 7 inches for working with a small number of stitches, 10 inches for average-size projects like most sweaters, and 14 inches for projects with many stitches. The 7-inch needles come in sizes 0 to 7, and are usually made from aluminum or plastic. The 10-inch needles come in sizes 0 to 15. They are made from aluminum, nylon-coated metal, plastic, and bamboo. For beginners, working with worsted-size yarn, I recommend the 10-inch aluminum needles, in size 9 or 10. They are easier to work with because they won't get in the way, and the aluminum is less likely to break.

The 14-inch needles range in size from 0 to 50. They are available in aluminum, nylon-coated metal, plastic, bamboo, and wood. The sizes above 19 look and feel like broomsticks! Unless you plan to make something that calls for making huge stitches using many strands of yarn at the same time, you probably won't use these needles much.

The world seems to be divided between knitters who prefer straight needles and those who won't use anything but circular needles. And knitters can be very adamant about their preferences. Circular needles are designed for working in rounds. They may also be used instead of straight needles for knitting back and forth on a whole bunch of stitches, or for knitting two parts at the same time. They have two rigid plastic or aluminum pointed ends, connected by a flexible nylon cord, and they are available in lengths from 6 inches to 36 inches. The short ones are used to pick up and work stitches around necklines, socks, or sleeves. The longest ones can handle enough stitches for knitting sweaters and skirts without seams.

I have found some disadvantages to circular needles. If they are not used often, the connecting coil can develop stubborn kinks. Also, stitches tend to catch on the connecting joins, which can distort them. And with the exception of the bamboo, circular needles are not marked for size. Circular needles can be handy for certain jobs such as picking up dropped stitches or holding cables, but they are just too much fooling around for me.

On the other hand, some knitters think straight needles are absolute abominations and should never have been invented. I've shared my thoughts, but don't take my word, and don't let anyone else influence your choice of tools. Find out for yourself. It's more important to be happy and enjoy the process than to be uptight about the tools. Your hands will soon let you know what's most comfortable and best for you.

Like circular needles, double-pointed needles are used to work in the round and may be substituted for them. They are pointed at both ends and are made from plastic or aluminum in sizes up to 11. You will need double-pointed needles if you decide to knit socks or gloves or anything where you must maneuver in a small space or make small rounds. Double-pointed needles are used in sets of fours or fives. The stitches are divided among three or four of the needles, and the remaining one is the working needle.

Jumper needles are circular needles that look as if they have been cut in half. The points are connected to a flexible nylon cord with a flat disk at the other end to prevent stitches from sliding off. They come in pairs about 18 inches long, in sizes from 4 to 15. Jumpers are used like straight needles and are particularly handy when traveling on buses or planes, where space is tight. They rest easily in your lap so they won't poke your neighbor.

A good, balanced needle collection should include a variety of needle sizes, in straight, circular, and double-pointed needles. Buy as many sizes and types of needles as you can afford, then add to your collection whenever possible.

Needle sizes are not consistent in every country. A chart comparing the U.S., British, and Continental needles sizes is in the appendix on page 136. In the United States, needles are sized from 00 to 50—the smaller the number, the smaller the needle. Older English and Australian needles were sized just the opposite, from 14 to 000—the larger the number, the smaller the needle. Continental needles, now generally used outside the U.S., are sized by their diameter in millimeters so the smaller the number, the smaller the needle. All three types are available at most needlework shops in the United States so the chart may be of help when you are outside of your comfort zone. When you are without a needle gauge, punch holes with your needles in a piece of paper and tuck it in your wallet. Then when you're traveling and lose a needle, you'll have an immediate size reference.

A palette of yarns

While needles come in a specific range of sizes and types, knitting yarns are almost infinite in variety. The endless choices of fiber, color, weight, and texture are what make knitting today such an exciting and creative pursuit. And it's this variety that makes it more important than ever for a knitter to be able to choose yarns with confidence and a spirit of adventure.

There are no seasons for yarns. Cottons are being worn in fall and winter, and wools in summer. Since the heightened interest in handknitting (and machine knitting as well), manufacturers are offering new yarns and colors several times a year, following the game plan of the fashion designers. But remember that knitting takes time. The project you start during one season might not be finished until the next. So forget about what season it is when you shop for yarns.

The constant introduction of new yarns can become confusing. It's like picking out wallpaper—after a while, everything becomes a blur. Knitting magazines recommend a specific yarn for a particular pattern, worked out by the designer. Then readers rush to the knitting shop clutching the magazine, looking for that yarn. Keep reminding yourself that one yarn can be interchanged with another for any reason, providing the stitch gauge remains the same.

Finding your way through the yarn jungle

Don't even think about starting a project until you shop around. When members of my group were planning their projects, they toured many yarn shops, touching and feeling everything, and reading the labels. You should pinch and squeeze and roll the yarn around between your fingers. Does it feel good? Is the color right? What about the texture? How will it work up in your design?

Most yarn shops will have samples on display so you can see how each yarn will look when knitted. This is very helpful, especially for beginners, because it is difficult to tell what a yarn will look like *until* it's knitted. The texture or color on the shelf may not produce the knitted fabric you anticipated at all. It is a good idea to invest in a few balls of the yarns you like and knit samples with several needle sizes, using the pattern stitches you have chosen.

Examine the yarn carefully. Just because a yarn is expensive, there is no guarantee it is high-quality, and less expensive yarns are not necessarily of bad quality. Will the yarn tend to split as you work with it? This is always a frustration because the split yarn might stand out in the finished material and look awful, in addition to weakening the fabric.

The cardigan on the right is an excellent example of what can happen if you don't knit a sample first. When I saw the yarn, I immediately had to have it. The color especially intrigued me; it was a muted brown heather, with tiny flecks of red, mauve, and soft green. I could wear it with everything. The yarn itself resembled spool knitting—it looked as if it were braided. And it was very expensive. Since I was traveling away from home, I bought all there was, to be on the safe side. Mentally, I'd already envisioned the design and could hardly wait to start knitting. The yarn seemed delicious to work with at first; it literally glided on the needles—except it split! I had to watch out for split stitches every minute. And the finished sweater catches on everything, causing the yarn to shred. Had I taken my own advice and knitted a swatch right away, I might have discovered these problems before buying so much of the yarn. It was a very expensive lesson.

Always read yarn labels carefully. I can't stress that enough. There is no consistency to the type of information that appears on labels, in part because so many of the new yarns are manufactured in other countries. Most will include the weight of the yarn,

recommended needle size, laundering information, the number of yards, and fiber content. The number of grams or ounces is not nearly as critical as the number of yards per ball or skein. Even then, the number of yards may vary slightly from one skein to another. Many manufacturers use a universal system of symbols easily understood anywhere in the world, much like traffic signs. Nevertheless, it's still important to ask lots of questions. Most other countries use the metric system, so I have included a chart in the appendix (page 136) to help

This distinctive plaid cardigan was made from heather-toned wool in warm brown tones with white mohair stripes. The vertical lines are slipstitch crochet in wool and mohair.

you convert grams and centimeters to ounces and inches.

Another problem to watch for is distortion. This can happen during manufacture when the yarn at the end of a batch is stretched as it is wound into the ball or skein. I learned about distortion when I was knitting a tunic sweater and noticed that one side seemed to pull at an angle. No amount of blocking helped the situation. Unraveling and reknitting the same yarn was no solution, either. Luckily I had more of the same color from a different batch, so I was able to reknit one side with the new yarn. This will happen occasionally; if it does, return the yarn for a replacement, and with luck, you'll find the same dye lot.

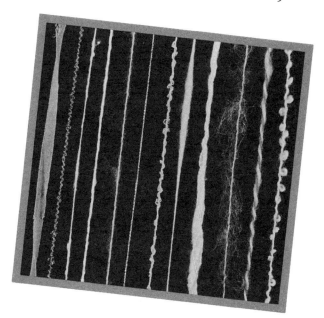

There is a multitude of yarns available to the handknitter today. Even strips of cloth can be used for interesting effects.

Yarn styles

Once upon a time, handknitters could choose from smooth, plied yarns in bulky, worsted, sport, or fingering weights. Those were the choices! Each weight of yarn could be knitted on two or three different needle sizes, depending on how loose or tight the knitter's tension was and how firm a fabric was wanted.

Today, yarns come in literally hundreds of different weights and styles. This is a bit mind-boggling until you discover, when you start to examine yarns closely, that even though there may be a huge variety of yarns to choose from, those from one manufacturer will invariably resemble those from another. Commercial patterns and designs in knitting magazines usually recommend a specific yarn. You need not rush to the knitting shop looking for that particular yarn. You can substitute one yarn for another as long as the stitch gauge is the same and the fiber types behave similarly in the ways that matter. So, again, it boils down to a matter of personal choice. Your feelings about color and texture are the prime considerations, not what someone else says must be so.

Fiber choices

For comfort and durability, the fiber content of a yarn is probably more important than its style. And fiber choices have increased in the last few years, especially in the ranges of cottons, silks, and luxury fibers. It's useful to understand where the different fibers come from and how they behave—whether they have any "give," whether they'll stretch out of shape, how easy they'll be to care for. Let's look at the characteristics of some of the more common fibers found in knitting yarns.

Wool. Of the protein fibers, the ones that come from animals, wool is by far the most popular. It has always been my favorite. In my opinion, it is the most versatile and trustworthy of all fibers. You will appreciate its elasticity, the wide range of colors and textures, its wearability, and of course, its warmth.

If you are a beginner, I recommend that you knit your first couple of sweaters from a basic smooth wool yarn, such as knitting worsted. You'll be able to see the stitches easily and it is relatively inexpensive.

Knits made from wools seem to be better looking and easier to care for than ever before. The soft, lightweight wool yarns, called "cool wools" by the Wool Bureau, Inc., can be worn in any climate, even hot tropical areas. Wool absorbs moisture and breathes so it doesn't stick to your body. Every year I spend a few months in Hawaii, where the average temperature is about 80 degrees. I wear my lightweight wool sweaters as often as those made from cotton or linen. In fact, because they're lighter, many wools feel even more comfortable than cottons or linens.

Of course, the shape of the garments makes a difference. Those I select for my Hawaiian trip are always loose and fluid, just barely skimming the body. People who live in desert climates, such as Egypt or India, wear loose, voluminous garments, often made from wool or wool combined with cotton or silk. The flowing shape and absorbency of the wool have a cooling effect.

I still have fond memories of a wonderful sleeveless dress and its companion coat made from knitting worsted. Because I live in Seattle, where the weather can be "iffy," it became a favorite ensemble. But I'll never know why I took the dress to Los Angeles one summer. Despite the 90-degree weather I found myself wearing it often because it felt so comfortable. While standing on a corner waiting for the light to change, a woman behind me reached out to feel the material. She apologized and looked rather embarrassed when I turned around. She just couldn't believe that anyone could possibly be wearing a knit, and from wool yet, in that heat. As we chatted, it turned out that she was a knitter, too, and I think she was convinced how comfortable and cool I was in that dress. I've often thought of that brief conversation and wonder if she ever experimented for herself.

The colors of most wool yarn tend to stay fresh and bright with two exceptions—white and some shades of blue. The whites may yellow a bit, but that's easily remedied by dipping the garment in a commercial whitener (but not chlorine bleach). And the blues may fade with frequent exposure to sunlight. These are minor inconveniences compared to the wearability of wool over a long period of time. And now that there are wool yarns that can be put in the washing machine and dryer, upkeep is easy providing you pay attention to the laundering instructions.

Besides the comfort and easy care benefits of wool, there are some other tidbits you should know about. Wool has an incredible memory and will return to its original shape; it resists pulls and tears and won't pucker permanently. Pilling is almost nonexistent in a good-quality yarn; when it does happen the pills are easily removed. Wool releases dirt when washed or dry cleaned better than other fibers do because its springiness helps prevent surface dirt from digging into the fabric. Wool has a built-in fire resistance—it doesn't melt and resists ignition. Wool fibers hold moisture and therefore ward off static build-up and do not cling as synthetics do. Firmly-knitted wool garments are water-resistant, shedding snow and light rain; and wool will hold its beauty longer than any other fiber. All of these properties make wool an economical and smart choice for handknitting.

It's a good idea to knit your first few sweaters with a smooth wool yarn. This sweater is a simple design with textural interest added by alternating blocks of stockinette and reverse stockinette stitch. The rolled neck is an easy variation to try.

"Cool wools" are lightweight, firmly-spun smooth yarns, such as those recommended for baby garments. Fabrics made from these yarns will shed wrinkles faster than you can find them. They won't wilt in warm weather and can take any shape and hold it, no matter how many times they are worn. They have all the characteristics of traditional wools and come in an infinite variety of colors and textures. Who could ask for anything more?

Handspun wools are very special and more available today in knitting weights than ever before. I love knitting with them. It's particularly intriguing to know that a real person sheared the sheep and carded and spun the wool, and often dyed it as well. In Mexico, I watched handspun wool being dyed by the most primitive method, in a huge metal cauldron heated over a wood fire. After the skeins of yarn were simmered for a while to absorb the dye, they were strung up on long poles to air dry. The day I was there the color was a lovely bright maroon with a softly mottled effect because the wool hadn't been heavily processed. I rather like the color and texture variations of many of the handspun, hand-dyed wools; they give garments character.

Many handspun yarns are made from wool which has not had all the natural oils washed, or scoured, out, making them more water-repellent for outerwear. When working with these yarns, you get a bonus—a lanolin treatment for your hands while you knit. But sometimes these yarns have a strong odor. Rinsing them several times in lukewarm water to which about 1/2 cup of vinegar has been added will usually remove the odor, but sometimes it never goes away.

Other animal fibers. In addition to wool, we knitters today can choose from cashmere, angora, alpaca, llama, mohair, and other even more exotic animal fibers. Some yarns from animal fibers are smooth, some crinkly, some are fat, some thin, some are both thick and thin. Some fibers have a soft, silky feel when you knit with them, others can be abrasive. In all my years of knitting with every type of animal fiber, from the very finest on little tiny needles, to the more luxurious ones, each has had a special quality. In my closet today are garments that have survived more than twenty years of heavy wear and are still going strong. Some have even been unraveled and reknitted more than once.

Silk. Silk, which is a protein filament produced by the silkworm, is the longest and strongest of the natural textile fibers. It is very fine and has a beautiful luster. Silk used to be considered a luxury fiber because only the rich could afford it, but it is now widely available and affordable, even if you're not a millionaire.

There are many varieties of silk yarns available for handknitting, including the characteristic smooth lustrous yarn, nubby textured yarns, and yarns spun from short silk "waste." Silk should be handled with care to retain its beautiful finish. It is less resilient than wool, so when considering a silk garment, always plan to knit to the finished size and add elastic to ribbings. Used by itself in a knitted garment, silk has little body and is prone to creep. If you are going to use silk yarn, think about combining it with a filler yarn for added stability.

The sweater on the right is made from a silk chenille *without* a filler yarn. When I first saw this exquisite yarn, it practically leaped into my arms. Originally I had planned to add a very fine, firmly spun Merino wool in a matching color. Because the wool was lightweight, I thought it would give just the right amount of body. Was I mistaken! After knitting up swatches of the silk and wool together on several sizes of needles, it was apparent that the wool, despite its fine weight, still overpowered the very qualities of the silk that

The silk chenille discovered in a weaving shop produced a soft, luxurious sweater. It features dolman sleeves, a rolled collar, and a vertical row of popcorns bordered by lines of gray and camel wool.

had caught my attention in the first place. I decided not to use the wool and immediately eliminated the idea of a matching skirt—it would never hold up. (Early experiences like this one are what taught me the importance of always knitting swatches first, before doing the planned garment. Imagine the time I'd have wasted.)

I discovered the silk chenille in a weaving shop. It came in great big hanks that had to be wound into balls. I discovered something else—it should not be wound with a commercial ball winder because the winder stretches and distorts the yarn. I also found that silk chenille sheds, so I kept a clean white towel draped across my lap when working with it. And the chenille had to be dry cleaned; washing removed too much of the original loft of the fiber.

Cotton, linen, and ramie. Cotton and linen yarns are available now that were undreamed of just a few short years ago— and in a dazzling array of textures and colors. They must be knitted to the correct size because they are fairly inelastic, but they are easy to care for and launder beautifully.

There have been valid complaints about some of the cotton yarns. After they've been knitted and worn a few times they begin to stretch badly. When people started complaining to me more frequently, I began to ask questions of people knowledgeable about textile production. I found out that cotton is a very short fiber—often just a fraction of an inch long—and therefore a cotton yarn, to be strong, must be tightly twisted. With a softly twisted knitting yarn, the fibers can begin to separate as a garment is worn, causing it to stretch. How is it possible to predict whether this will

This oversized sweater blouse, made of alternating panels of rectangles, has dropped shoulders and a bateau neckline. It was knitted with cotton slub and silk in stockinette stitch with a ribbed hem. Inset: Two rectangles sewn together in opposite directions.

happen? Only by applying the torture test. Before you knit, work up a good-sized sample with the same needles you intend to use for the sweater. Wash it a few times and let it dry naturally. Leave it out in the sun to check for fading. Press it to see if it still keeps its shape. Measure your sample before and after and make a note of any changes in size, shape, or color. Your test results will indicate whether you want to work with the yarn.

Linen, on the other hand, is so strong, and the fibers so long, that it usually retains its original shape, except when knitted in ribbed cuffs, necklines, and hems (which are easily fixed by weaving in several rows of elastic thread). Linen can keep you cool in hot climates and it is also comfortable in cool climates—I wear my linens all year. Other fibers—cotton, silk, and even wool—are often combined with linen. Weaving shops usually have a good selection of linen yarns in a broad range of colors and textures. Linen yarn is usually wound on cones or spools and may be purchased by the ounce or half ounce. Be aware that dye lots are rarely identified on coned linen, so buy as much as you'll need for a garment, plus a few ounces more, just in case.

Ramie, also known as China grass, is a bast fiber like flax, from which linen is made. It is obtained from the stingless nettle plant. Other bast fibers may be more familiar to you—they include jute and hemp. Although ramie has been around for more than a thousand years, U.S. manufacturers have only recently begun to use it extensively.

Ramie has characteristics similar to linen. It takes dye easily and is very strong. It is often used with other fibers as a strengthener. Ramie yarn, like linen, has a high luster and is absorbent and dries quickly. What a boon in this hectic, fast-moving world!

Ramie is not a resilient yarn. It also wrinkles, but since wrinkles are "in" these days, that's not a big drawback. Some ramie yarns aren't very lightfast, either. Try it yourself, if only to satisfy your curiosity, and then make up your own mind about ramie.

Black and white cotton yarn is suitable for any season. The white abstract inserts are rayon ribbon and appear on both sides of the sweater, making it a turnabout.

Man-made fibers. Rayon is a man-made fiber that has a lot of the properties of cotton and silk. Because it is derived from cotton lint and wood chips, it's often regarded as being in the same class as the natural fibers. There are several types of rayon and all have slightly different properties. Acetate is also derived from cotton lint and wood chips, although the process is different from that used to produce rayon. In general, rayon and acetate are fairly easy to take care of, but they wrinkle like crazy.

Synthetic fibers, on the other hand, are made from petrochemicals. As a class, synthetic fabrics do not breathe and they usually pill easily. They can melt under heat, and stains may be difficult to remove from them. They are strong, however. Have you ever tried to break a strand of synthetic yarn? Your fingers will break before the fibers will.

There is no fooling around with synthetic yarns—they must be knitted to fit. And if you need to unravel, the kinks are permanently set. In some cases, it's hard to tell the difference between a man-made and a natural-fiber yarn by sight and feel. Read the labels carefully and you'll find that man-made fibers are often used in combination with many of the natural fibers.

I call man-made yarns "pretend" yarns and usually try to avoid them. They do have their place, though, especially when knitting for children. But, oh, do they pill! The outfit below, worn by my granddaughter, Stephanie Dore, is made from a very inexpensive, machine-washable, worsted-weight synthetic. Knowing that her mother prefers clothes that can be thrown in the washer, I deliberately chose this yarn. She'll probably outgrow it before it pills. Besides, I happened to have just enough in my knitting bag.

Stephanie is adorable in her red and blue jumper with matching leg warmers. They are made from four-ply synthetic yarn for easy care. (See also pages 129–131.)

Knitting Vocabulary

Because terms are repeated frequently, a system of abbreviations has evolved to describe hand movements and to identify special techniques. The system is fairly consistent everywhere in the world. All commercial instructions use these abbreviations, with some variations, depending on the country of origin. For example, in some countries the word wool is used instead of yarn. Generally, pattern books include a list of the most frequently used abbreviations.

alt—alternate

approx—approximately

b—back of work

beg—beginning

bet—between

bo—bind off; finish the knitting by pulling one stitch over another, locking it in place to prevent unraveling

cc—contrasting color

cn—circular needle

co—cast on stitches; put the beginning loops on the needle

col—color

cont—continue

dec—decrease the number of stitches

dpn—double-pointed needle

foll—following

g st—garter stitch; knit every row

inc—increase the number of stitches

k—knit stitches; put the needle into the front of the loop on the needle and bring the yarn around the needle

kb—knit back; knit in back of the loop

k1B—knit a stitch in the row below the next stitch

k2tog—knit 2 stitches together

lh—left hand

lp—loop; the folded yarn that forms the basis for all knitting

mc—main color

n—needle

no—number of stitches or rows to be worked

p—purl stitches; put the needle into the loop from back to front and bring the yarn over and under the needle

pat—pattern(s)

pb—purl back; purl in back of the loop

psso—pass a slipped stitch over a worked stitch

p1B—purl a stitch in the row below the next stitch

p2tog—purl 2 stitches together

r—row

rem—remaining; the pattern or stitches left to be worked

rep—repeat; repeat the stitch or pattern

rev st st—reverse stockinette stitch

rf—front of work facing you

rh—right hand

rib—ribbing

rnd—round; when working with circular needles, one round equals one row on straight needles

rpt—repeat

rs—right side

sk—skip

sl—slip; slide a stitch from one needle to
the other without working it

sl lp—slip loop

ssk—slip, slip, knit

st(s)—stitch(es)

st st—stockinette stitch (U.S.); stocking
stitch (Eng.); knit one row, purl one row

tbl—through the back loop

tog—together; knit two stitches together

ws—wrong side

wyib—with yarn in back

wyif—with yarn in front

yo—yarn-over; put the yarn around the
needle to make another stitch

There are several other terms and symbols
that appear in knitting instructions:

as if to knit—insert the needle from front to
back of a stitch; the English term is
knitwise

as if to purl—insert the needle from back to
front of a stitch; the English term is
purlwise

left edge—the left edge facing you, but
actually the right edge of your garment

right edge—the right edge facing you, but
the left edge of your garment

right side—the outside of the garment when
it's finished

wrong side—the inside of the garment
when it's finished

work even—work without increasing or decreasing; the English term is work straight

asterisk (*)—asterisks are used to surround
a group of stitches or lines in a pattern
that are to be repeated; for example,
k2tog

parentheses—additional sizes or stitches are
put in parentheses; for example, size 10
(12) (14)

These three summer goodies were easy to design and knit. They are timeless designs that can be worn for a variety of occasions. Instructions for the Rainbow Sweater, left, are on pages 114–117; instructions for the White Slipover, right, are on pages 122–123. The camisole, center, is also featured on page 98.

Chapter 2
WHAT ABOUT GAUGE?

Each time I start another book, I think, "This time it won't be necessary to dwell on gauge because all knitters know that gauge is the single most important thing to know about knitting." But important messages are worth repeating, so I'll say it again: I can't stress enough the importance of knowing how to figure and use gauge. Should you get just 1/2 stitch more or less per inch than you anticipated, your sweater will be 3 or 4 inches wider or narrower, and may not fit.

Those who attend my workshops must demonstrate that they really do understand gauge. Once the mystery of gauge is peeled away, knitting is a breeze. In a workshop in Honolulu, everyone worked a sample of stockinette stitch with different sizes of needles. To help identify the differences, a couple of rows of garter stitch were knitted between each change of needles. Then each person measured gauge for me. There were new knitters as well as experienced knitters in the group, and more than half had trouble identifying and measuring the changes in gauge. We worked for quite a while until that little light bulb went on and everyone felt confident and understood what was happening.

A friend of mine is a super knitter who knits constantly. She must have the latest of everything but complained to me that nothing ever turned out right—her garments were either too big or too small. My first question was, "Do you make a sample swatch and check the gauge before you start?" She told me it was a waste of time because she was anxious to start. Well, waste time she did, because she was constantly unraveling. She also never bothered to measure the gauge as her knitting progressed, to check for consistency.

I'm not saying you'll never have to rip if you watch the gauge, but be assured it will happen less often if you stop for a couple of minutes every 3 or 4 inches to measure. It's your mileage check. If you can do simple arithmetic—add, subtract, multiply, and divide—then you can control gauge, and you're the boss of your project.

"Why is it necessary to measure so often if I've already worked out a sample?" you ask. Because if it's been a stressful day, your knitting will reflect it by tightening up. When you're in a hurry, there might also be a change. Even the weather could be a factor.

Needles of the same size may vary from one manufacturer to the next. To test this, I knitted a swatch with plastic-coated needles from two different companies. There was fully 1/2 stitch difference between the two brands of size 6 needles. Then I knitted another swatch with size 6 circular needles from the same two manufacturers. The circular needles produced a slightly different gauge than the straight needles. So you see, you just can't take anything for granted. Also avoid using two different kinds of needles (such as aluminum and plastic) as a pair, because the gauge will be slightly askew from one row to another. This may not always be crucial, but it's safer to work with matching needles so you don't have to be constantly on the lookout for discrepancies.

When you create your own design, you're the one who will decide whether a stitch gauge is right for the project. Once the yarn has been chosen, work up a sample using several different sizes of needles, and then decide which is most appealing to you.

After you've chosen the gauge, then it's time to knit a larger swatch to test the consistency of your gauge. The best time to knit your gauge swatch is when you are relaxed and comfortable, with no distractions. For example, to make a 6-inch square sample with a gauge of 5 stitches per inch, cast on 30 stitches. Knit until the piece measures 6 inches vertically. Check your gauge again. Are you still getting 5 stitches per inch? If the measurement is more than 5 stitches per inch, try larger needles; if it's less, try smaller needles. Remember, it's the number of stitches per inch that's important, not the size of the needles.

If you'll be working with two or more different types of yarn, determine the gauge for each type. Even different colors of the same yarn might produce a slightly different gauge.

And what about pattern stitches? If you plan to include a pattern stitch, be sure to measure for that gauge, too. If the pattern is an openwork stitch, then the knitting could very well be much looser. A small area of openwork won't make much difference. But test, test, test. Be alert.

If you intend to include more than one pattern stitch in your design, take time to make a sample that includes the stitches as they will be used in your garment. Measure the swatch horizontally to see if the stitch gauge has changed or if you should make some adjustments. At this point, if the patterns don't seem to work together you may decide on a different combination. Now's the time to find out, instead of starting your garment and finding out halfway through that the result wasn't what you'd intended. This has happened to me more times than I care to admit. My stubbornness made me continue and I was unhappy with the whole project. So benefit from my mistakes.

When you measure, be sure to avoid any stretching or pulling of the stitches, because this will surely give an incorrect gauge. Measure in the middle of the swatch, not up against the cast-off edge (or against the needle if you haven't cast off yet). Prevent the sample from slipping around by laying it on a towel; the nap of the towel helps to anchor the material. If you don't have a metal knitting gauge, use a tape measure.

Knitters become very opinionated about the tools they work with, and I bow to that. We each have our own special way of working, with very definite preferences about tools. One professional knitter I know is adamant against using those metal rulers with the cutouts. She says they are not accurate for determining gauge. I happen to like them and have never had a problem. You should decide for yourself.

Once you are satisfied with the gauge and

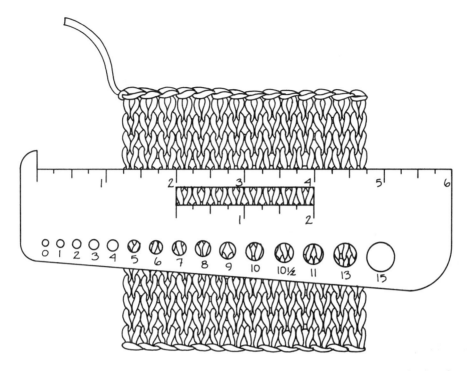

To determine gauge, count the number of stitches in a 2-inch section in the middle of your swatch. Don't forget to divide this number by 2 to get stitches per inch.

have started your project, knit a couple of inches and measure again. If there's too much material to lie flat while still on the needles, run a piece of string or contrasting color yarn through all the stitches and slip them off the needles. Has the gauge remained the same, or is there a difference? If you're on target, continue knitting, otherwise change to larger or smaller needles as required to maintain the intended gauge.

Another safety measure that works for me is to knit the back about halfway up, then knit half of the front. Spread both parts out and hold them up to your body. Do they look as though they'll fit? Is your stitch gauge consistent?

Still a bit unsteady about planning from "scratch"? Give yourself a little test. Make a simple drawing and write in your measurements in the appropriate places. Then according to your stitch gauge, calculate the number of stitches needed at each of the crucial stages—waist, hips, upper thighs, and approximate length and bottom circumference for a skirt; underarm, width at bust, length from shoulder to hem, length and width of sleeve for a top. Write these on the drawing with your measurements. This will show you where and how often any increasing or decreasing should occur and helps you to visualize how gauge can work for you.

I haven't touched on vertical row gauge,

mainly because only in rare instances does it become a concern. However, I do get many letters from readers who have fits because a printed pattern might call for 5 stitches per inch and 6 rows vertically, but no matter how many swatches they knit, the vertical measurement is never the same. The vertical measurement can be controlled by knitting more or fewer rows, so it's not terribly crucial. It's much easier to make an adjustment vertically than horizontally.

Don't begrudge what might seem "overkill" about testing and measuring. The precautions in this chapter are valuable and will add to a joyful knitting experience. You'll see.

This bold graphic ascot was designed to be worn with the cashmere/alpaca outfit on page 34 and the cover. Matching accessories add a special flair to handknitted garments, and they're a great way to use up leftover bits of yarn.

Chapter 3
PLANNING AHEAD

What do you do when you travel to another country? First, you make the transportation reservations so you'll be assured of reaching your destination; then you reserve a place to stay so you won't have to sleep in the park. After you arrive, you arrange all the other things, like visiting castles, seeing museums, staking out the shops, and meeting the people. Those who are more adventurous may just pack up and take their chances. There is nothing wrong with that, because the element of surprise can lead to some wonderful experiences.

But whatever your persuasion, some initial planning can help avoid problems. The same holds true in knitting. Don't just jump in and begin knitting. First, picture your design. Think in terms of the whole project, not just bits and pieces. Details such as trim and pockets may change along the way, but you will at least have in mind an idea of the final design if you do some initial planning.

Some basic decisions

Get out your notebook and make a list of all the things you expect to accomplish with your design with regard to your figure, your wardrobe, and your budget. I still do this after having knitted hundreds of garments. It helps avoid frustration and disappointment. Your list might include:

1. Type of garment—pullover, cardigan, skirt, jacket
2. Shape of the garment
3. Body features you want to disguise
4. Proportions you'd like to improve
5. Type of sleeve you prefer
6. Type of neckline that flatters
7. Color/colors
8. Texture
9. Other clothing you want to mix and match with
10. Cost

Take this list with you when shopping for yarn. If you can't find a yarn that will work with most of your requirements, keep looking. The right combination will happen, and you'll be a lot happier for having thought ahead.

The same care and thought should go into choosing the type and color of yarn and the shape of a garment as you would give to choosing shoes or other parts of your wardrobe. Will the handknitted garment reflect your own personality and lifestyle? Will it work for more than one occasion? Will it go with at least three or four other things in your closet? It's a fairly simple matter to buy clothes (and to return them if you have second thoughts), but handknits take a lot of time and effort and should be considered special.

Unfortunately, many knitters don't plan ahead much. Emotion often governs their choices—something caught their eye in a magazine, or the color seemed intriguing at the time. A strong emotional response can often cloud the vision, and I'm as guilty of this as anyone. My closet harbors its share of impulsive purchases that turned out to be disasters.

Developing your ideas

To begin, you need to establish a fairly good idea of what you want to knit. First, decide on the shape of the garment. There are as many shapes for knits as there are for any other kinds of clothing, and you can control the shape as you knit. To help you visualize the shape, make a little drawing. It doesn't matter whether or not you can draw—no one will see it but you. If you need help, check the stores for what's happening fashionwise. Try on a few garments to see how you feel in them. Try shapes and styles that you don't usually wear, too. If you've never worn a blouson top because you didn't think it was "you," you may change your mind when you see how flattering it can be. Something similar happened to one of the members of the knitting group. When Jo began to plan her outfit, she was reluctant to deviate from her usual conservative style. After trying on some of my oversized sweaters, she discovered that not only were they comfortable, but they made her look slender, as well.

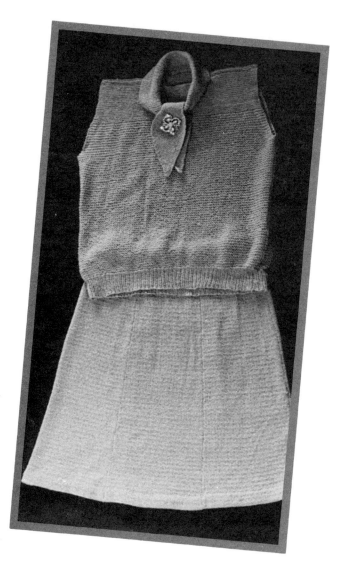

Jo's sleeveless sweater vest was knitted in fine wool with decreasing needle sizes from bottom to top. It has an attached ascot and a matching six-gore skirt.

And how do you feel about color? Remember, you'll not only be wearing it, but you'll be working with it for a while, too, so make sure it's a color you can live with. Maybe you're thinking it would be interesting and fun to include more than one. You're tall enough to handle a bulky sweater made with two or three colors, and maybe a companion skirt knitted from a slightly lighter weight yarn. You've already established that your main color choice can be worn with other garments. The bulky yarn you've chosen has an uneven texture, and it will knit up quickly. But you're still not completely convinced; there's a nagging negative hovering in the back of your mind. Before you lock yourself in, buy a ball of that yarn and work up a good-sized sample. This will tell you right away whether you like working with it and if the color distribution is what you had expected. If it doesn't work out, tuck that ball of yarn in your knitting bag. You'll think of something else to do with it.

Jackie decided to knit a three-piece ensemble for a pulled-together look. She is very petite so it was important to consider the weight and texture of the yarn as well as the color. She chose a beautiful mauve mohair for the pullover top, with a coordinating skirt knitted from a smooth wool. Because the mohair was such an unusual color, she wisely decided to keep it simple in order to emphasize the beauty of the yarn, and used an open pattern stitch for interest at the neckline. Mauve is a difficult color to match or blend with, so rather than make a hasty decision about the coordinating jacket, she worked on something else for a while and then went back to the mauve with a fresh perspective.

How do you like to feel in your clothes?

If you're a teen, then you're probably running fast, and your clothes must allow you plenty of movement and must be fun to wear as well. Knits can do that. Fashion changes almost minute by minute, but good design endures. No longer are we bound to those days when clothing clutched at the body and tight sleeves practically cut off circulation. So choose designs that you feel comfortable in and that reflect your lifestyle.

Jackie's mauve mohair pullover has an inset yoke of open eyelet stitch that makes for a simple, attractive neckline. The four-gore A-line skirt was knitted from mauve wool in stockinette stitch.

Choose carefully—you'll hate yourself and the whole project if you don't. And don't let anyone talk you into something you're not comfortable with. It just won't work! My friend Mary had an unpleasant experience at a yarn shop. Mary is usually secure in her decisions, besides being a very skilled knitter. She was almost backed into a corner by the salesperson, and finally ended up buying a particular yarn. She knitted it up and hated everything about it. To this day she has never worn the garment.

That's not to say you should ignore advice. Listen, evaluate, take your time, and then let the final decision be yours. You'll be a happier knitter if you do. I'm offering you some tools—use them wisely.

How much yarn do you need?

In general, I have found that a long-sleeved sweater in a worsted-weight yarn uses about 1300 yards of yarn. A cardigan requires about 1500 yards, depending on the fullness of the sleeves and the length of the sweater. A skirt may take about 1600 yards of worsted-weight yarn, depending on length.

Here's a more precise method for figuring yardage. Once you have selected your yarn, knit one whole ball or skein with the needles and the pattern stitch you intend to use, then measure the number of inches vertically and horizontally. This will tell you how many square inches you'll get from one ball or skein.* (Don't forget to work out the stitch gauge before you make your garment, because if you decide to change the gauge, the amount of fabric will also change.) Based on the measurements you'll be using for your design, this should give you a pretty close idea of the amount of yarn needed. Don't forget that extra couple of balls in case you decide to change some part of the design midstream. That's the fun of inventing your own design—you can give yourself permission to change your mind whenever it suits you.

Skirts require a bit of extra consideration. They are subject to a different kind of stress than tops—we sit, stand, walk, run—so the fabric should be a firmer knit than the top. For instance, if you plan to use a size 10 needle for the sweater top, try a size 7 or 8 for the skirt. This helps to prevent that "rump sprung" look. Planning a heavily textured sweater? Then look for a smoother yarn to blend with the top.

Some knitters are too stingy about buying yarn. They hate to buy even one extra ball or skein. When they run out, or a hole needs repairing, or they decide to change the design, they will be in trouble. On the bright side, if you do run out of yarn before the sweater is finished, and no more is available, tap your creativity. You may have to add a stripe, even though you hadn't planned one.

---

* If your yarn comes in larger skeins and you don't want to knit a whole one for a sample, knit a swatch that's 8 or 10 inches square, and then unravel it and measure the number of yards that it required.

Chapter 4
BECOMING YOUR OWN DESIGNER

When I owned a yarn shop, not a day went by without someone coming in clutching a commercial pattern, wanting to buy the exact yarn specified for that particular design. This timid knitter wouldn't have a clue as to whether the color would flatter her, whether the yarn would be a pleasure to handle, or even whether the pattern design and the weight and texture of the yarn were appropriate for her figure. After the garment was completed, then would come the disappointment, with the sweater ending up in the back of the closet, never to be seen again. She had let a nameless designer make her choices for her.

Choosing the right shape, color, and texture are especially important for successful, happy knitting. How many times have you seen a commercial pattern that seemed so appealing, right down to the exact yarn and color specified, only to discover after you'd completed it that it was completely wrong? Based on my own experience as a designer and former owner of a yarn shop, I think I can speak with some authority, having heard all of the horror stories, with a few of my own thrown in as well.

Understanding proportion

Many disasters with handknits might have been avoided if a few basics about proportion had been learned at the beginning. Most of us don't want to think critically about our bodies. But let me tell you, good proportion and some yarn smarts will help you accentuate your good points while camouflaging the other ones. Fashion designers are particularly concerned with proportion, for this element can determine the success or failure of their designs.

What is proportion? Proportion is spacing—the relationship of parts to each other and to the total. It has to do with how one section of a total design relates to another, such as the length of the skirt to the dimensions of the bodice; or the fullness or slimness of a skirt compared to the length of a sweater or jacket. Imagine your figure is a rectangle. Now mentally cut that rectangle in half. The two parts have a blocky appearance. The trick is to choose lines that divide the top and bottom in more interesting ways.

How does one determine good proportion? Following are some guidelines that professional designers use. As you begin to recognize your own figure characteristics and develop an idea of basic design elements and how they work, you can use this information to achieve pleasing proportions. Because of the very nature of the fabric, it is easy to manipulate proportion in knits once you understand a few basic rules.

The drawing on the right shows a figure with average body proportions. Confidentially, I don't know who originated these "average" proportions, but they are accepted as standard in the fashion industry. The following principles hold for the *average* body:

1. Across the shoulders and from the nape of the neck to the waist is equal.
2. The waist is the midpoint between the underarms and the widest part of the hips.
3. Elbows rest at the hips.
4. The hips are the midpoint of the vertical body measurement.
5. The tips of the fingers fall at about the middle of the thigh.
6. The knees are midway between hips and toes.

Write down your own measurements beside the appropriate areas. Measure yourself from time to time to be sure your body measurements have not changed, especially if you have a younger body that is still developing. Noting these measurements on the figure that best represents your body type on page 29, or on a sketch of your own, will give you a pretty good idea of how close you are to average, and what features you want to draw attention to or away from in your clothing designs. Don't be concerned if you're not average. Nobody is. You're special, and your handknits should be special, too. The idea is to create knitted

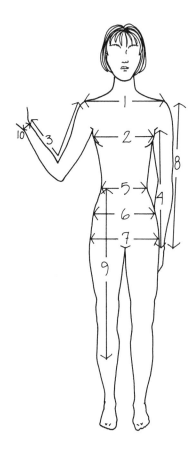

Figure with average proportions.

Record your own measurements for the following:
1. *Shoulder width*
2. *Bust*
3. *Arm length—bent*
4. *Underarm length*
5. *Waist*
6. *Midpoint between waist and hip (at the hipbones)*
7. *Hip*
8. *Arm length—straight*
9. *Skirt length*
10. *Wrist circumference*

fashions based on your *own* proportions. By choosing the right shapes, colors, and fabrics, you can create the illusion of a well-proportioned body—and that's what fashion design is all about.

To help you make a correct diagnosis of *your* figure, have a friend help you with some measurements. Let's forget about feet and inches, and think instead about proportion, using the height of your head as the basic unit of measurement. The one measurement that doesn't ever change, even if your weight does, is the how many heads tall you are. No matter what your actual height might be, the average adult figure is somewhere between 7 and 7½ head heights tall. (It's a couple fewer for kids.) For your

head-height measurement, use a yardstick (not a tape measure), and measure from the top of your head to the bottom of your chin. Take off your shoes and stand up nice and straight. From the bottom of your chin, measure down the rest of your body to your toes. Add these two figures for a total height measurement. The total height will most likely be about 7 or 7½ times the head measurement. Check it out—it does add up.

Note how many "heads" down your waist and other key figure elements measure. Look at the drawing below to see how different figure types are proportioned in relation to the seven-head rule. Which figure type is similar to yours?

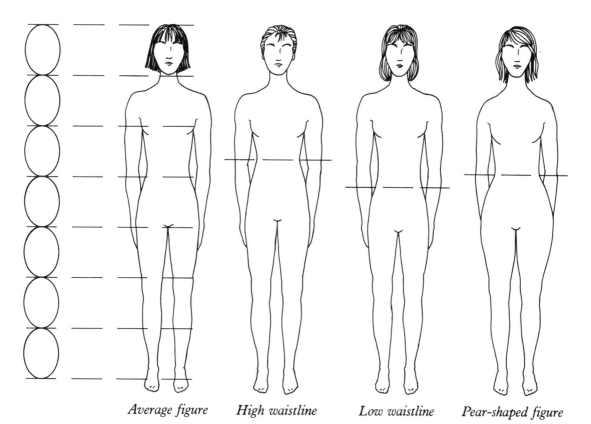

Average figure   *High waistline*   *Low waistline*   *Pear-shaped figure*

Because proportions will change with different heel heights, take your measurements with two or three different sizes of heels and record them. With each increase in heel height, your proportions will change: your upper body will be shorter relative to the waist-down measurement.

Having an objective mental picture of your own body proportions is the key to designing knits that will enhance your figure assets. Let's consider a hypothetical figure. This figure is about 5'4", with a short waistline, broad shoulders, long arms and legs, and full hips. What should be emphasized and what should be disguised? The broad shoulders, coupled with a full bustline and short waistline, present a bulky, boxy image, with toothpick arms and legs.

I would plan a sweater or ensemble that flatters by minimizing the bust and short waist. This is done by elongating the body of the sweater so that the hem falls at the hip. The person with this figure should steer clear of tops designed to be tucked in. They will emphasize the heavy bust and the end result will look as though the whole body were being shoved up to the shoulders. An exaggerated V-neck will pull the eye down, drawing attention away from the heavier bustline. This hypothetical figure has long legs, so an A-line skirt in a longer length will also give the illusion of height and a longer body line.

Our hypothetical figure has long arms, too. For long arms, add some extra fullness above the wrist, or at the elbow. A straight, generous sleeve, stopping an inch or two below the elbow, or narrowing in width below the elbow, or narrowing in width down to the wristbone, can help to minimize the length. An interesting pattern treatment at the upper arm would be another solution.

If I were designing for this figure, I would choose a monochromatic color scheme and use a simple stockinette stitch for the skirt. I would use an overall pattern for texture in the sweater, and perhaps I would add a touch of color somewhere on the sleeve and around the neckline. I might also pick up the yarn colors with a bright print scarf or add some interesting jewelry.

To make intelligent design decisions, train yourself to view your own body with sharp, critical eyes. Stand in front of the mirror stark naked. Remember that being honest with yourself at this stage will prevent grief later on. Think about what needs to be camouflaged and what should be emphasized.

Do you think your hips are too big for the rest of you? Then plan a design with some interesting detail at the neckline to draw the eye away from the hip. Is a small waistline one of your best features? An unusual belt or pattern stitch will call attention to it. Do you have narrow hips and think that you can't wear knits well? Try an overblouse, belted at the waist and paired with a full skirt. In other words, once you've learned to identify your figure "pluses" and "minuses," you'll be able to plan flattering shapes for your handknits. No matter what your figure type, you can successfully create and wear beautiful handknits. The rest of this chapter covers some ideas that embellish, enhance, or disguise specific figure characteristics.

Creating illusions

People with high waistlines seem to have a difficult time buying ready-made clothing. I've always had a problem finding well-fitting garments, because quality, fashionable, ready-mades do not cater to those of us with this figure problem. Almost everything I buy needs extensive alterations. You can imagine my delight when I discovered the ease of knitting to my own measurements.

I have found that the long torso line is an effective device to give the illusion of length and balance. If you are high-waisted, go to your favorite store and try on some designs featuring a dropped waist. Not only does this design elongate the figure, but it can hide a multitude of other figure problems.

Long-waisted people have problems, too. One way to break up that long expanse of torso is to add interest at the natural waistline. The eye will be drawn to that area of the garment rather than to the blank expanse between the shoulder and waistline.

If you have a tiny waist and large hips, you may tend to emphasize your waist. Instead of calling attention to your tiny waist, which is out of proportion to your larger hips, design a sweater top to overlap your skirt or pants, then add a narrow belt that falls about at the top of your hipbone.

The right-hand figure on page 29 is usually referred to as pear-shaped. If you have a figure like this, I recommend using light and zingy colors, with an emphasis on broadening the shoulder line and drawing the eye up and away from the heavier part of the body. Plan a top that ends above the fullest part of the hip, with no break in color, or one that falls well below the thigh. A skirt with some fullness below the knee will balance the proportion. A basic cardigan or sweater jacket covering the fullest part of the behind with some interest near the shoulder line will help to smooth out the line of the body.

Create the illusion of broader shoulders with knit shoulder pads. The Joan Crawford look keeps slipping in and out of the fashion picture—exaggerated shoulders narrowing down to slim hips. Store-bought pads have always seemed too rigid for knits, so I make my own from scraps of leftover yarns or from matching yarn. The pads I knit add just a bit of shape, and they mold nicely over the shoulder. Experiment to see if they'll work for you.

To steer the eye away from a heavier waistline, an elongated sweater with a narrow band of openwork around the neckline immediately draws the eye upward. Use a pattern stitch in a vertical line down the middle of the sweater and continue it down the length of the skirt. The vertical pattern insert will give the effect of height.

Unless you are tall enough to carry it off, avoid a decorative skirt hemline, especially in a contrasting color. This will appear to cut you off at the knees. If you enjoy color contrasts and want to liven up your knit, think "vertical." Use shades of the main color—something that blends—to give a light and shadow effect.

Heavy upper arms were a concern of many of the group—young and old alike—so we spent some time talking about ways to camouflage them. In the old days, sweaters featured tight-fitting sleeves that fit like the skin on a hot dog. Not only were they unattractive, but they were uncomfortable and inhibited free arm movement. Some of those relics still live in my closet. I think I save them just to remind me how much I

Shoulder Pads

With size 11 needles and 3 strands of yarn, cast on 3 stitches. Work in garter stitch, and increase 1 stitch every other row until there are 25 stitches. Place a marker before the center stitch. On the next row, knit across until 1 stitch before the marker. Slip that stitch and the center stitch together to the right hand needle, knit 1, pass the 2 slipped stitches over the knit stitch, complete the row. (The 2 slipped stitches passed over the knit stitch form a little hump which gives the pad its shape.) Continue increasing every other row until there are 29 stitches. Repeat the decrease, and at the same time continue to increase 1 stitch every other row, until there are 31 stitches. Work another decrease at the center stitch. Knit one row even, then bind off.

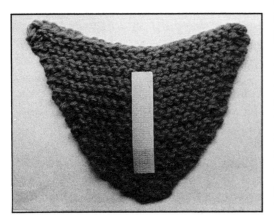

To make larger pads, follow the same sequence as described above, increasing at each end every other row, and decreasing at the center on the opposite side. For thicker padding, sew two pads together.

To fasten the pads to your sweater, you have a couple of choices—they can be permanently stitched to the shoulder of the sweater, or the "hook" side of a piece of Velcro,® stitched to the top of the pad, will hold the pad firmly in place. It will adhere to the knitted material without damage and the pads are easily removed. I don't recommend the sticky-back Velcro® for knits, so be sure to buy the kind you sew on. I prefer removable pads rather than the permanently stitched-in variety, so they can be used for more than one sweater.

Blousy raglan sleeves with ribbed cuffs are comfortable and fashionable.

Zigzags on the sleeves are one way to add textural interest (see page 57 for information on how to create zigzags or slants).

appreciate the relaxed and comfortable feel of the new sleeve treatments. Once you've tried the new sleeves, you, too, will enjoy that free and easy feeling. And just as important, you'll enjoy the ease of planning them.

Almost every design in this book features a version of these comfortable, easy sleeve treatments. They're so "right" for today's busy, frantic world. And age has nothing to do with it. If your arms are very thin, or you think they're too heavy, a tight-fitting sleeve will only call attention to them. To satisfy my curiosity, I spent several days checking out clothing in department and specialty stores. Almost none featured those complicated, old-fashioned, set-in sleeves.

The easiest sleeve of all is a straight rectangle, which can be knitted any length you choose. Roll it up at the hem, or wear it as is. It can be converted to a blousy sleeve by adding elastic or a ribbed cuff at the wrist. Add some texture by running a zigzag down the center, or include a narrow pattern stitch border. This straight sleeve will slide nicely into an L-shaped armhole; it may also be sewn to the sides of a garment with no shaping. Specific instructions for knitting sleeves can be found in Chapter 5.

Do you want to disguise heavier hips and thighs, or are you very short? Then don't even think of a patterned skirt. The skirt on page 34 is an example of a big "no no." Don't ask me why I ever designed this skirt, except as an exercise in futility. Although it's a match for the sweater, I'm only 5'2", and it not only cut me in half visually, but the flamboyant arrangement of color wiped me out. The yarn is luxurious cashmere and alpaca, and someday I'll unravel it and design something else. Meanwhile, it serves as a constant reminder of what *not* to do. On the other hand, a very tall, slender person could certainly carry this strong design.

With a heavier bustline, avoid such trimmings as allover fringes. They'll just draw attention to the part you want to disguise. Instead, work with color and pattern above that area and no one will ever notice the rest of you. Vertical stripes of blended colors, in a low-texture pattern stitch will add some height.

Add a ruffle around a neckline to conceal a less-than-perfect neck. Pick up stitches around the neck edge. On the next row, increase in every stitch on that row, and every right side row two or three more

Ruffles around the neckline and on the sleeves are charming on this cotton sweater knitted by Florence, one of the members of the group.

times, until the ruffled edge is as deep as you desire. That's all there is to it. Do the same at the sleeve cuff; eliminate the ribbing, and add the ruffled edge by picking up stitches after the sleeve is completed. The ruffle will hide a bony wrist, and at the same time, add some flare to an ordinary sweater.

No matter what your figure type, you can successfully create and wear flattering knits, provided you become familiar with proportion. You will be positively amazed at how flattering knits can be. You have absolute control when you design and make your own handknits. Take advantage of the unlimited ways to disguise and create illusion, and make your knits your own personal statement. Illusion doesn't cost a cent, but it can sure make an enormous difference in the overall effect. Before long, your personal sense of proportion and design will become automatic.

Let illusion and disguise work for you.

It takes a special type of figure to wear a large-patterned skirt like this cashmere/alpaca two-panel skirt.

Chapter 5
A BASIC TOP AND SKIRT

T-shaped sweater

The tops described in this chapter are based on a simple "T" shape, which will fit anyone. The shoulder drops slightly, and no special fitting is necessary. A decided advantage is that this design is comfortable and arm movements aren't restricted. And a new knitter will be able to make a successful sweater the first time out with this simple design. It lends itself to a variety of sleeve and neckline styles, not to mention endless variations in color, texture, and trims. The front and back are knitted flat as two separate pieces, and the sleeves are set into the straight side seams. What could be simpler?

To design your own T-shaped sweater, first plan how long you want it to be from shoulder to hem. Decide how deep an armhole opening will be comfortable for you. Use a sweater that fits as a guide. For example, let's say that the armhole depth is 10 inches plus 1/4 inch for the shoulder seam—10¼ inches total. Knit the front and back pieces straight up from the sweater hem, shaping the neck front according to the neckline you want. (See Chapter 8 for neckline suggestions). Place a safety pin or yarn marker 10¼ inches below the shoulder, at the edge of each section. With

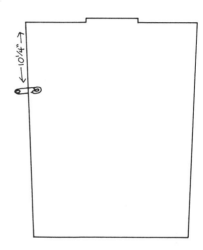

Marking depth of armhole.

right sides facing, sew the front and back shoulders together. Open the two sections, lay them out on a flat surface, and measure the distance between the yarn markers. The distance between the markers, *after sewing,* should be 20 inches. With a gauge of 4 stitches to the inch, multiplied by 20 inches, there should be 80 stitches around the sleeve when the sleeve is completed. Plan your sleeve to fit that opening.

Check the diagram showing your body measurements, and start knitting at the wrist. Again, this is only an example. If

36

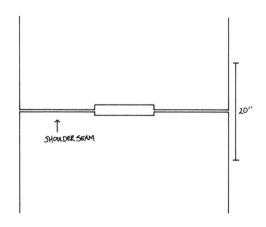

20"

SHOULDER SEAM

Marking off for sleeve.

your wrist measures 8 inches, and the gauge is 4 stitches to the inch, then you would cast on 32 stitches for the cuff. Make the cuff as deep as you want—we'll say 3 inches. For a blousy sleeve, on the next row, increase 1 stitch in *every* stitch (64 stitches and 16 inches wide). You need add only 4 more inches (or 16 stitches) to reach the final width of 20 inches, or 80 stitches. You have 16 inches above the cuff in which to add the additional stitches. Since each stitch is equal to 1/4 inch, you should increase one stitch each side every 2 inches, 8 times. This gives you a total of 80 stitches when you've reached a sleeve length of 19 inches, including the cuff. Bind off loosely.

Do you like your sleeves longer? Work *even* after the last increase to the desired length. For a shorter sleeve, add the additional 16 stitches more frequently—about every 1½ inches. Each time you increase 1 stitch at each side, you add 1/2 inch to the width of the sleeve. Therefore, 1/2 inch

multiplied by 8 will add the additional 4 inches, for a measurement of 20 inches at the armhole edge of the sleeve.

Check the drawings again to be sure you understand how it all works. It's really pretty simple.

What if you want to make a *narrower* sleeve and armhole? It works the same way. First decide how deep you want the armhole. Let's say this one will be 8 inches deep. Place your markers at the point on the front and back pieces 8¼ inches down from the shoulder (including 1/4 inch for the seam), or 16 inches at the armhole edge after sewing the shoulders together. The gauge is 4 stitches to the inch. The wrist measurement is 6 inches, and the total length of the sleeve is 18 inches. So, you'll cast on 24 stitches for the cuff. You still need to add 40 more stitches for a 16-inch measurement at the top of the sleeve, and you have 15 inches in which to add those stitches. Increase 1 stitch each side every 3/4 inch, until 40 stitches have been added (for a total of 64 stitches). Fortunately, absolute precision is not crucial with the no-shape armhole and sleeve, so if you are a row or two short of the desired length, work those additional rows even. If you have an extra couple of rows, just push up your sleeve a bit, or fold back the cuff. That's what I do.

The perfectly straight sleeve is easiest of all. First decide on the depth of the armhole and the number of stitches, and work even until the sleeve is whatever length you want. Bind off.

For a puffed or dimpled sleeve, add 2 or 3 inches to the top sleeve width. Pin the top of the sleeve to the armhole, right sides facing. Start pinning at each outside edge toward the center, to within 2 inches each side of the shoulder seam. You'll have a big bunch of material. Ease the remaining material by placing the pins closer together. Try to make the gathers as even as possible. After all the pins have been positioned, *baste* the sleeve edge to the armhole before you sew to prevent the gathers from shifting around.

Even though this sounds like a broken record, it bears repeating—don't go into a tizzy about that extra stitch or two. Knitted material can be wiggled around and made to fit. Just don't let it scare you.

Don't you hate it when the cuffs of your sweater sleeves stretch out of shape? Here's a happy solution that works for me. Weave three or four rows of elastic thread through the inside of the cuff. Use a tapestry needle to do this after all the parts have been connected. At the bottom of the cuff, starting at the seam edge, weave the elastic thread through the back loop of every second or third stitch, around the cuff and back to the seam. Draw the elastic in until your hand slides in and out easily. Work the needle over the last stitch a couple of times to fasten it firmly. When you push up the sleeves, the cuffs will stay in place. Sneaky, huh?

To make a simple gathered sleeve, short or long, just eliminate the ribbed cuff. After all the seams have been sewn, fold the bottom edge of the sleeve under about 1/2 inch, and slipstitch in place with matching yarn. Catch just the loop of the stitch so the stitching won't show on the right side. Measure off a narrow strip of elastic to fit your wrist or arm, and slide it through the hem. Sew the two ends of the elastic together, and that's all there is to it. Instant gathered sleeve.

Skirt

A skirt is a skirt, is a skirt . . . but no knitted skirts, thank you. That was the general consensus of the group when we first began meeting. One member, who particularly enjoyed working intricate pattern stitches, felt she might be bored to tears because nothing much would happen to hold her attention. Another was convinced she could never wear a handknitted skirt because of her generous figure. Even Eleanor, who is extraordinarily slender, thought a knitted skirt seemed like an impossible project. Almost everyone seemed to have a built-in resistance. We discussed skirts for quite a while, and eventually, I brought out several handknitted skirts, each a different shape, color, and texture. After a trying-on session, attitudes began to change, especially when group members saw the feasibility of having a complete outfit—that fit. Very soon, everyone in the group was including a skirt in her knitting project.

A carefully designed handknitted skirt is suitable for any figure, and especially so if your figure is less than perfect. The shape can be easily controlled as you knit. This is not true when working with woven material—any adjustments in width and length must be completed before cutting into the material. Then if you goof, the whole thing may have to be discarded. A handknit can be unraveled and reknitted without harming the yarn, and you have the freedom to change your mind whenever you please.

My strong opinions come forth again when it comes to skirts knitted with circular needles—I think they're the reason women are so resistant to the idea of wearing handknitted skirts. They tend to look tacky, unflattering, and homemade, rather than handmade. All the necessary decreases interrupt the smooth flow of the material, to say nothing of the zillion stitches that must be struggled with. Talk about boring!

A knitted skirt should flow easily in order to hang well, so plan your skirt at least 2 inches larger around than your actual body measurements. No matter what design you use, work in sections from waistline to hem, then sew all the parts together. The seaming prevents the material from clutching at your body and also acts as a stabilizer to keep the fabric from stretching. All the skirts in this book can be knitted in sections on straight needles. Many are A-line, which anyone can wear. The A-line may be made with two, three, or four panels, or even more.

Other skirts are variations of the classic A-line, such as the flared skirt, with all the fullness falling from just above the knee, or the softly flared skirt, with modified fullness. The pleated skirt on page 43 is essentially a two-panel straight skirt, with the pleats allowing extra movement at the knee.

Be sure to consider your proportions when planning a skirt. And there are other details to keep in mind as well. How will you move in it? Will you be sitting a lot? Will the skirt yarn match or coordinate with the sweater yarn? What color should it be?

If your sweater yarn is thick or uneven in texture, find a lighter weight yarn for the skirt. A bulky yarn will appear to add inches to your figure and the skirt will not hold its shape very well. To pull the look together, add a touch of the skirt yarn somewhere on the sweater, perhaps around the neckline or as a stripe in the sleeves.

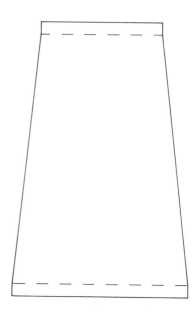

The front and back of a two-panel skirt are the same.

First, knit a good-sized sample swatch with the yarn and needle size you've selected. How does it look? Does the material seem firm enough to hold its shape? Try a couple of other needle sizes and compare the results. You might find yourself using a smaller needle size for a skirt than you would for a sweater in the same yarn. When the texture pleases you, measure the stitch gauge. The successful fit of your skirt will depend on that gauge. Make a simple drawing and write down the number of stitches necessary for the waistline, hip, heaviest part of the thighs, and around the hem; then determine the approximate length. If you're uneasy about these measurements, find a woven skirt that fits the way you like it. Draw an outline of it and compare those measurements to yours.

Now make a casing for the elastic in the waist. For a two-panel skirt, multiply the number of inches around the waist by the stitch gauge. For example, a stitch gauge of 4 stitches per inch, multiplied by a 26-inch waist measurement, gives you 104 stitches. Divide this figure in half (because there will be two panels) to get 52 stitches, then add an extra stitch at each side for a seam allowance. This gives you 54 stitches, the number of stitches you will cast on. Work 1 inch even, knit in back of every stitch in the next right side row, knit 1 inch even. This will make a casing for elastic.

As a general rule, the hip measurement is about 10 inches larger than the waist measurement. This is only a general rule—your own measurement may be more or less. To add the additional inches for the hip, it is necessary to increase one stitch on each side, every few rows from waist to hip. In our example, because 10 additional stitches must be added on each side between waist and hip, you would increase one stitch each side every inch, 10 times. When you get to this stage, hold the skirt up against your body to be sure it fits.

Next, increase the number of stitches until you reach the planned width and length. For a skirt that measures 42 inches around the hem, increase to 21 inches for the front, and the same for the back, by increasing one stitch at each side four more times. Be sure to keep the increases evenly spaced. Knit even to the desired length, knit a turning row (knit in the back of each stitch on a knit row), change to a needle one size smaller, and work even for another 1 to 1½ inches for the hem. Bind off loosely to prevent the stitches from breaking or the hem from puckering. If you have trouble maintaining a loose tension, bind off with a larger needle. Do the same for both front and back panels.

After both panels are completed, with right sides of the material together, pin, baste, then backstitch the seams with matching yarn, easing the material in if necessary. If the yarn seems too thick to form a smooth seam, separate the strands, if possible, and use a single strand for sewing. Fold the waistband to the inside and carefully slipstitch in place. Be sure the stitch tension is as close to the knitting tension as possible. Leave a small section unstitched so elastic can be inserted. Turn back the bottom hem to the inside at the turning row, and slipstitch.

If you have heavy hips, plan a three-panel A-line skirt. The same method is used to calculate the number of stitches for this design except the back is divided into two equal panels, joined with a straight center back seam. This design is flattering because the center back seam reinforces the fabric so it won't cling to the body and thus helps to eliminate unsightly bulges. The total number of stitches for the two back panels should equal that of the single front

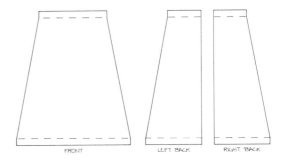

Three-panel skirt.

panel, plus two additional stitches for the center seam allowance. All of the increases are done at the two side seams and the center seam remains straight. Work both back panels as if you were knitting two sleeves at the same time, to assure that all increases will occur on the same rows. For more fullness below the hipline, add two or three more increases 12 to 14 inches above the finished length.

With right sides facing, sew the two straight edges of the back panels together first. Then follow the procedure described for a two-panel skirt.

Designing your skirt. Knitting a skirt seemed an awesome task to most of the group at first. However, once they understood the simple arithmetic, and where the increasing should occur, almost everyone began to plan a skirt.

Barbara decided that bias stripes would emphasize her beautiful alpaca yarn. The skirt and sweater are knitted in stockinette stitch, in shades of ivory and camel. The skirt is made in two panels, with the bias stripes meeting at the center. After the skirt was finished, she discovered that when she turned the side seams to the front and back, the V's changed direction. Now she turns her skirt front to back and side to side, to distribute the wear and tear.

Muriel ran into some trouble with her four-panel design. At first she decided to work the increases by using two methods—escalating the size of the needles, and at the same time, adding side seam increases. The skirt kept getting bigger and wider and she couldn't figure out why this was happening. Finally she discovered that as she changed

Barbara's bias skirt can be worn with the V's at the side or in the center. The coordinating polo shirt has bias stripes on the sleeves.

needle sizes, the stitch gauge changed dramatically, so she was getting fewer stitches to the inch. After unraveling her work a couple of times, she was ready to forget the whole project. Rather than see that happen, we talked about possible ways to retrieve her efforts and avoid unraveling again. I suggested she leave the panels as they were, and put them all on a yoke by picking up stitches at the top of the skirt and working up to the waistline from there. The extra fullness she was so distressed about would then fall at the hipline. The yoke, knitted in the opposite direction, would add a contemporary look. This simple adjustment proved to be the answer, and the skirt fits her

beautifully. It also proved that ingenuity and a sense of adventure, with a willingness to accept risk, resulted in an even more attractive skirt than she had anticipated. She was thrilled.

Bev had originally decided she wanted a pleated skirt to match her sparkly sweater. Because she had never knitted a skirt before, I suggested she think "flare" before tackling a more complicated design. She chose a six-panel skirt, with the fullness starting just above the knee. Bev is tall, so the additional fullness was a good balance for her proportions.

To plan a six-panel skirt, divide the number of waistline stitches by six, and add two stitches to each panel for seam allowances. Follow the procedure described earlier for the two-panel skirt, increasing according to your stitch gauge. About 4 to 6 inches above the knee, start increasing more frequently for a more definite flare.

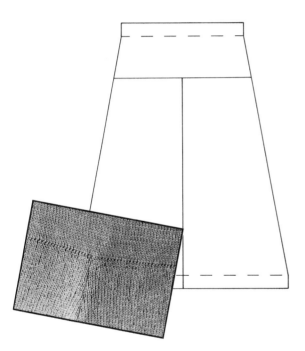

Muriel's yoked skirt. Inset: Detail showing attachment of yoke.

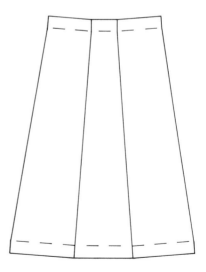

Six-panel skirt.

Beverly's six-panel skirt of wool and lurex with matching sweater.

Pleated skirts never seem to go out of fashion, and today they're more popular than ever. A lighter weight yarn with a smooth texture works well for this type of skirt. A heavier weight yarn will cause the pleats to sag, and the sheer weight of the yarn does not lend itself to a crisp pleat. The skirt on the right is made from a lightweight, smooth wool. The pleats are stitched down from the waist to just above the knee. The skirt should fit smoothly and fall gracefully down to the top of the pleats. Forget about intricate pattern stitches for this skirt because there's enough going on as it is, and they would only detract from the design.

The pleated skirt is knitted in two identical sections with extra allowance for the front and back pleats. According to your stitch gauge, divide the total waist measurement in half, and add 4 more inches of stitches for each panel. For example, for a waist measurement of 28 inches, divide that in half to get 14 inches, and add 4 more inches to get 18 inches. For a gauge of 5 stitches per inch, you would cast on 90 stitches. The center pleated panel should have 50 stitches and the two side sections, 20 stitches each. These pleats will measure, including the fold, about 2 inches. Make the pleats as deep as you wish, but be aware that the deeper the fold, the more thick material you'll have across your midsection. The pleats in this skirt are about 6 inches apart at the waistline after they are folded. To avoid a wide expanse across your tummy, the pleat stitching should fall about

This skirt with topstitched pleats was knitted from a lightweight "cool wool" in stockinette stitch.

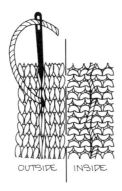

OUTSIDE | INSIDE

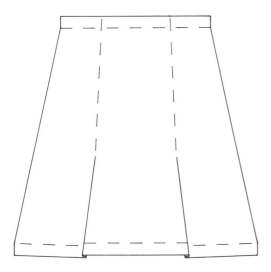

Pleated skirt. Above, topstitch the pleats in place before sewing the side seams.

according to your proportions, whether or not it will flatter your figure. The tiers may be positioned as far apart as you wish, with each successive horizontal panel a bit fuller than the previous one. The fullness is achieved by doubling the number of stitches on one row, working a knit row on the purl side, and on the next right-side row, immediately decreasing the number of stitches back to the original number. At the same time, gradual increases about 1½ inches apart are worked at each side seam edge all the way to the hem. The skirt shown is made in two identical sections, and may be worn front to back to distribute wear.

To plan a tiered skirt, determine the number of stitches to cast on according to your measurements and stitch gauge. Then decide how wide apart you'd like each panel. A good rule of thumb is to plan each panel about 6 inches in depth, evenly spaced, according to the desired length. If

2 inches in from your hipbone on either side. Stitch the pleats before sewing the side seams. Slipstitch the waistband and hem to the inside. This skirt may also be worn front to back.

If you want a soft, casual look, the tiered skirt may be the one for you. The extra, graduated fullness may not be suitable for everyone, however. You'll have to decide,

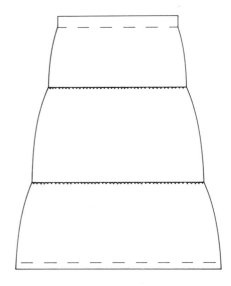

Tiered skirt.

you are short, perhaps narrower panels would be more in scale for your height. Cast on the appropriate number of stitches for one panel, starting at the waistline. Knit 1 inch even, knit a turning row, and knit another inch. This is the waistband. Begin the side increases about 1½ inches down from the bottom of the waistband, then increase about every 1½ inches. When your work measures 6 inches, on the next right side row, increase 1 stitch in every stitch. *Knit back.* On the next row, knit 2 together all across the row. You have completed the first tier. Knit as many tiers as necessary until the skirt is the desired length. Instead of a conventional hem, a few rows of single crochet will help the skirt hang well. Or a knitted picot hem will make a tiny scalloped edge. If you would like more fullness, immediately after the increase/decrease rows have been completed, increase several stitches evenly spaced along the next knit row.

To avoid bulk, choose a lightweight yarn for this design. This skirt may be easily adapted for a child, too. Follow the same procedure, and as the child grows, add more tiers.

There are many schools of thought about hemming knit skirts. My personal preference is a turned-back hem, except when the yarn has so much texture that the fold is not crisp and defined. In this case, a crocheted edge would be appropriate. Sometimes just a row of single crochet is adequate, but if the skirt is knitted from a lightweight cotton or linen, several rows of crochet may be necessary to make the skirt hang well.

You now have several skirt designs to consider—and I hope you will become as addicted as I am to knitting skirts that go with your sweaters. No matter what your size, age, or shape, you can knit a skirt that fits.

Chapter 6
THE GRAND SWITCH

There is an old miner's card game in which one of the plays is called "the grand switch." It is legitimate for the player to move the cards around from one position to another in order to win the hand. In the fickle world of fashion, there is a similar concept—it's called separates. Where would we be without separates? Our busy lives demand versatile clothes. Mixing, matching, and layering are practical tools for extending our wardrobes. I'm a firm believer in making clothing do double, sometimes triple, duty. Who can afford to buy or knit an outfit and wear it only for special occasions? In my opinion, it's especially important to make careful decisions when planning handknits.

Combined creatively, knitted separates are top-drawer wardrobe extenders, no matter what your age or lifestyle. With a couple of basics like blouses and slacks, they'll take you from early morning to late evening, and you'll always be well-turned-out.

Do you plan your clothing or are you an impulse buyer? We're all guilty of bowing to impulse sometimes, especially when it comes to choosing yarns and designs. We're beguiled by color or texture, but fail to consider whether our choice will blend in with what we already have in our closets. Then,

This versatile ensemble is great for taking on trips. The three-piece outfit was knitted from Australian wool and mohair.

45

after the garment is finished, we discover that the result doesn't work with anything else we already have. The rest of this chapter is devoted to a description of how I put handknitted garments together in ensembles that work for me. Once you begin to seriously evaluate your wardrobe and plan your knitting projects around it, you, too, can get a lot more mileage from your clothing.

For instance, a basic V-neck pullover, worn with a matching or coordinated skirt and a classic cardigan, will provide at least four, and perhaps more, variations. The three-piece ensemble on page 45 includes a warm, oversized jacket that can be worn over two or three layers, an elbow-length pullover made from the same yarn, and a modified A-line skirt. The predominant yarn is a gray Australian wool, and the contrasting yarn is a variegated brown mohair. The jacket is knitted from side to side and features vertical slash pockets. The pullover, knitted on large needles, may be worn over a shirt or, for dressier occasions, with a silk scarf or lots of necklaces. The simple, gored

The jacket from the ensemble on page 45 was knitted from side to side. It features a stand-up collar with tab, vertical patch pockets, double front facings, and dolman sleeves. The body is stripes of mohair in garter stitch alternated with Australian wool in stockinette stitch.

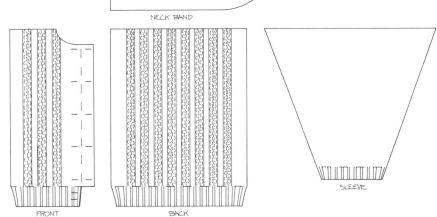

NECK BAND

FRONT   BACK   SLEEVE

skirt may be paired with several different tops in contrasting colors; the jacket can be worn with the matching skirt or with other skirts or pants. All three pieces worn together as an ensemble can take you anywhere. Because I travel extensively, I've often made these three pieces my primary outfit, adding a couple of neutral silk shirts, a pair of pants, a scarf or two, and some fun jewelry. Best of all, no pressing is ever necessary, no matter how long the outfit spent in my suitcase.

Another three-piece ensemble that always travels with me to warmer climates is shown on the right. The skirt features six gores and is somewhat full for easy movement. The cardigan is the classic V-neck golf sweater with dropped shoulders and full push-up sleeves. The short-sleeved pullover is just a hair oversized. I knitted this outfit more than 15 years ago and it's still fashionable. Over the years the only change I made was to remove the elastic thread from the bottom ribbing of the cardigan so that the sweater hangs freely, giving it a more contemporary look. I also knitted a yoke for the top of the skirt to make it longer. The yarn is a lightweight combination of synthetic and rayon, completely machine washable and dryable. The pastel apricot color is so neutral that it blends beautifully with several other pieces in my closet. When I'm in the mood, I slip in soft shoulder pads. I often pair the cardigan with a crisply pleated cream-colored skirt and a pastel print silk shirt. The smocking across the shoulder of the cardigan offers a bit of texture to an otherwise plain knit. Just for fun, the smocking is sewn with an intense pink double-strand embroidery thread.

This lightweight three-piece ensemble is over fifteen years old and still going strong.

The ensemble below was also designed to be worn several different ways. It is made from a fine-weight wool yarn—single-strand for the skirt and crew-neck pullover and double-strand for the V-neck pullover. The crew neck sweater was knitted with an open stitch, except for the ribbed cuffs, hem, and neckline. The V-neck pullover can be worn with a tailored skirt or pants for a casual look. The pleated skirt can also be worn with a blazer and turtleneck sweater.

The sweater on page 119 is made from four rectangles, knitted double-strand from a shimmery, hot pink, slightly textured rayon. Although there is a touch of multi-colored abstract design knitted into the fabric, it may be paired with a print skirt as long as the print is not too blatant and picks up the color of the sweater.

Who would have thought we would be mixing plaids and prints, flowers and stripes? It's not uncommon these days to see mixtures like these. The younger set knows how to switch their wardrobes around. They mix and match like crazy and somehow seem to come out beautifully, although sometimes a bit of guidance in choosing a shape would come in handy. Be adventurous, but not wild. Remember, when you knit garments, you're not only spending money, but time.

A handknitted tunic will be an asset to your wardrobe and will cover a multitude of woes. The tunic sweater below is a classic round-neck cardigan made in rectangles and knitted on size 11 needles. The sleeves are slightly shaped. The yarn, knitted double-strand, is a cotton/rayon/wool blend in off-white with slubs of orange, lavender,

The three pieces in this ensemble were designed to be worn in a variety of combinations.

A basic sweater like this cardigan tunic sweater can be a versatile addition to any wardrobe.

yellow, and mint green. I pair this sweater with an off-white wool pleated skirt and light-colored hose and shoes, and it can be worn for any occasion. I sometimes wear the sweater front to back and invariably, someone asks why the pockets are in the back. Just for fun—no other reason. People have even slipped coins in the pockets.

The twin sweater sets that were so popular in the fifties are making a big comeback and offer a variety of possibilities for mixing, matching, and layering. The sleeveless sweater may be worn as a vest over a shirt. For cooler days, add the cardigan. As the weather warms up, peel off the cardigan and the pullover or wear the sleeveless sweater alone. The sweaters need not be of the same color. Make the cardigan from one color and the sleeveless sweater from a coordinating color, then add a touch of the same color to both sweaters as a neckline trim or stripes. (See pages 126–127 for instructions for making sweater twins.)

Those who travel a great deal have learned all the tricks about mixing and matching so that it's almost automatic, even when the trip is a short one. Have you ever wondered how some people travel all over the world with only one suitcase? Before I pack for a trip, I pull several sweaters out of the closet, some skirts, a couple of pairs of pants, and two or three blouses. I spread these all over the bed and take a good look at them. Then I choose one basic sweater that will go with everything. Whatever else I choose must either blend or match with that sweater. Seeing everything laid out gives me a different perspective than when they are hanging in the closet. Sometimes things work together in combinations I hadn't considered before.

A good rule of thumb is to have at least one outstanding classic, made from high-quality yarn. Then you can get away with less expensive blouses and accessories; all the attention will be focused on the sweater.

Because I rarely need formal evening wear, almost everything I own can be classed as a separate. I like being able to switch my sweaters from front to back, so many of my pullovers have one detail on the front and another one on the back. This makes them fun to wear and I don't have to worry about putting them on backwards. A couple of my sweater designs can even be worn inside out. Playing turnabout with your knits saves wear and tear on them.

Your willingness to experiment with mixing, matching, and layering will offer new avenues of dress that may not have been evident in the past. It takes some thinking on your part, but the results are certainly worth it. Spice up your thinking and your wardrobe at the same time!

Once you begin to seriously evaluate your wardrobe and plan your knitting projects around it, you'll get a lot more mileage from your clothing. By thinking "separates" you can achieve an incredible versatility, especially if your budget is limited. You will, however, need to invest some thought to pull things together. Maybe some of those boo-boos you've knitted and thought were unwearable can be resurrected and mixed and matched. You'll come up with lots of possibilities once you train yourself to think "switch."

This summer eyelet is an example of the limit-less possibilities that await you when you design your own handknitted garments. Let your imagination wander. The bodice is knitted with a variation of the openwork stitch on page 53, and two types of ribbing make up the sleeve cuffs, hem, and bodice top.

Chapter 7
PATTERN STITCHES

Lately commercial knitting patterns seem to focus on gobs of pattern stitches. Many of those designs seem overdone to me, as if they are intended to test your technical skill. I call it "kitchen sink" designing. More is not necessarily better.

I'm not condemning the use of pattern stitches, but I do think that beautiful hand-knits needn't yell and scream for attention. As a designer in the fashion world might say, the idea is to make a statement with understatement. Why clutter a luscious yarn and beautiful shape with a hodgepodge of texture if it truly does nothing for the design itself? Now this doesn't necessarily apply to the Irish knits or some of the Fair Isle patterns, because there are historical reasons for those combinations of stitches. But please note that those sweaters are knitted from lovely, smooth wools, and the patterns are the focal point. It's fun to knit pattern stitches and to include some of them in your designs, but choose them wisely. It's often best to leave well enough alone and let the yarn speak for itself.

When I design a garment, the shape, color, texture, and beauty of the yarn are the primary features, and I include pattern stitches only in small doses—when a touch of pattern will add zest to the shape of the garment, or when a simple pattern stitch

will enhance the design. Most of the time I prefer a simple stockinette stitch to let the beauty and color of the yarn shine through. Besides, I don't like to plow through 32 lines of text to produce one pattern sequence—it slows me down and interrupts the creative flow.

The selective use of pattern stitches can enhance your knitting, but the only criterion for using a stitch should not be that it intrigues you. Ask yourself these questions before putting those first stitches on the needles:

1. Will the stitch texture mask the beauty of the yarn?
2. Will the stitch pattern overwhelm the shape?
3. Will the stitch be compatible with your proportions?
4. Will the techniques become a chore instead of a joy?
5. Will you be tired of it after wearing the garment a few times?

The group tossed these questions around for a long time. A couple of the group members who enjoy the challenge of intricate pattern stitches realized that the stitches could, indeed, detract from other design elements. Their final designs reflected their change in thinking.

Before making a final decision about your design, try the stitch or stitches with the yarn you've selected. Knit each pattern stitch with several different sizes of needles—perhaps a couple of inches in each needle size. This mini-test will immediately tell you whether or not you'll be happy with the results, or whether you'll even like working that pattern. Keep the samples in your notebook for future reference and write down your reactions. Make it a habit to check your notebook before you start each new project.

How I wish I had had the sense to follow this advice in my early days of knitting. It would have prevented many headaches and hours of frustration. Now, whenever I plan a new design, I automatically make notes of the pros and cons and consider it time and effort well spent.

Follow the directions for the stitches I've included in this chapter, making samples as you go along. They are easy to do and will provide subtle textures without overshadowing the beauty of the yarn or the basic shape of the garment. In addition to working these stitches with different sizes of needles, try them with two different needles used as a pair, just to see what happens to the texture. You'll have some surprises—some will be successful, some won't. And don't be concerned about the names of the various stitches. Depending on what book you happen to be looking at, the same stitch might be tagged with a different name.

Sand stitch

The sand stitch is a combination of plain knitting and knit 1, purl 1 ribbing, which

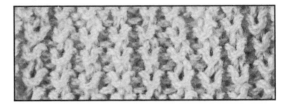

Above the right side of the sand stitch. Below, the opposite side.

gives it a nubby texture. Try this stitch at the hem of a sweater instead of conventional ribbing. It has less elasticity than ribbing, so make a mental note of that before including it in your design. The flanged vest on page 107 shows the sand stitch used as ribbing along the hem. Both sides of the pattern are equally interesting. The other side of the stitch has a pebbled surface which might be an interesting texture for a garment to be worn as outerwear, made with bulky smooth yarn or double strands of a medium-weight yarn on larger needles. There are just two rows to remember for this pattern stitch, and it's easy and fun.

Cast on an even number of stitches.

Row 1: Knit every stitch.
Row 2: *Knit 1, purl 1*. Repeat the stitches between the * * across the row. End with purl 1.

Brioche stitch

Here's another alternative to conventional ribbing. The brioche stitch is very elastic and holds its shape well. These two rows, worked alternately, produce a rather dense rib which looks the same on both sides. Knitting in the row below elevates the stitch. This stitch, worked as an overall pattern, is very handsome for a basic pullover or cardigan. It resembles commercial "Shaker" knits.

Cast on an even number of stitches.
Row 1: Knit.
Row 2: Knit 1, knit 1B (knit 1 stitch in the row below).

Above, openwork stitch.
Below, variation of the openwork stitch.

Openwork stitch

This is an open eyelet stitch that lends itself beautifully to summer garments made from silk, cotton, or linen. And it's also attractive when knitted with wool. Worked in metallic yarns, it's really a knockout! The sweater on page 54 is a basic crew neck pullover made from a lightweight wool knitted completely in this open stitch, with reverse single rib for the cuffs, hem, and neckline. This easy, versatile pattern stitch may be used to make a picot edge, for tiny buttonholes, or to provide an opening for a drawstring.

Cast on a multiple of 3 stitches, plus 2 stitches for each edge. The 2 edge stitches make it easier to control the seams.

Row 1: Knit.
Row 2: Knit 2 (edge stitches), *k1, yo, knit 2 together*, knit 2.
Variation: Work every row as row 2.

Bands of brioche stitch.

The entire sweater is knitted in the openwork stitch for a lacy effect.

Zigzag eyelet inserts are eyecatching.

Cobby stitch

This nubby stitch has a firm, dense texture, very appropriate for outerwear or a garment that requires a solid fabric. When knitted on large needles, size 10 or larger, the weave opens up. If you have been timid about working with more than one color, this stitch provides an easy introduction to working with two colors at the same time. Two shades of the same color will give a subtle color change.

To dramatically alter the texture, work rows 2 and 4 in purl instead of knit—it produces a vertical pin-stripe effect that can be very handsome when fashioned into an appropriate shape. Try this stitch with several sizes of needles. You'll be delighted by the variations that are possible.

Work with an even number of stitches and two colors, A and B.

Row 1 (right side): With color B, knit 1, *knit 1, slip 1 with yarn in back*. Repeat between * *. End with knit 1.
Row 2: With B, knit 1, *slip 1 with yarn in front, knit 1*. Repeat between * *. End with knit 1.

Cobby stitch.

Row 3: With A, knit 1, *slip 1 with yarn in back, knit 1 in back*. Repeat between * *. End with knit 1.
Row 4: With A, knit 1, *slip 1 with yarn in front*. Repeat between * *. End with knit 1.

Blocks of cobby stitch alternated with blocks of stockinette stitch, each worked in different colors, produce a high-low texture enhanced by the color scheme. First, calculate the number of stitches you'll need for the body of the sweater. Divide this number by the number of stitches you'll need for each block. Then alternate blocks of cobby and stockinette stitches. You may want to introduce a third color for the cuffs and hem. By alternating this way, you've added texture and color without a lot of complicated instructions to follow. You might also knit a cardigan in stockinette stitch and make pockets and trim with the cobby stitch. Make the sweater band from the cobby stitch, then sew it on after the sweater is completed. Or you can knit it at the same time you knit the two fronts. Don't forget to check your gauge because this stitch is much firmer than plain ribbing or stockinette stitch.

Open fan stitch

This stitch has an open, airy feeling which I particularly like. Try it with a lightweight mohair, as I did in the sweater below. The color of that sweater is a very bright orange, with a simple dropped shoulder and full, blousy sleeves. Had I used a firmer pattern stitch the sweater would have weighed a ton and been almost too warm to wear, so I invented this yarn-over stitch. But the laugh was on me—someone else had already invented it.

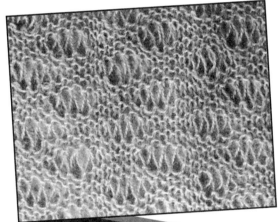

This mohair pullover was knitted with the open fan stitch. The cuffs and hem are brioche stitch.

The stitch is made by increasing, then decreasing, the number of yarn-overs over 5 stitches. Garter stitches at the beginning and at the end of the row, and between the open spaces, form the background. On every fourth row, the open segments are positioned so they fall in an alternating sequence. Try a sample with 20 stitches to start. This will give you 2 open segments plus 2 plain garter stitches at the beginning and end of the row, with 4 garter stitches separating the open areas. For the next group, begin the yarn-overs after the second garter stitch.

Rows 1 and 2: Knit.
Row 3: Knit 3, *yo, knit 1, yo twice, knit 1, yo 3 times, knit 1, yo twice, knit 1, yo, knit 1*, knit 4. Repeat between * *. End with knit 3.
Row 4: Knit, dropping all yo's.
Row 5: Knit.
Row 6: Knit 2, *yo, knit 1, yo twice, knit 1, yo 3 times, knit 1, yo twice, knit 1, yo, knit 1*, knit 6. Repeat between * *. End with knit 2.
Row 7: Knit, dropping all yo's.

Repeat these seven rows until your sample measures 6 or 8 inches. This is a large enough sample to give you a pretty good idea of how the yarn-overs alternate from one row to the next. Don't be timid. If you feel like varying the number of knit stitches between the open sections, go ahead. Or vary the number of rows between the yarn-over rows. Experiment with different combinations of open and solid knitting. The sweater on page 120 has yarn-over sections plunked in randomly whenever the spirit moved me. If you've never tried yarn-overs like this, wait until you see how much fun it is. And don't be frazzled when the yarn-overs are dropped from the needle—they won't go anywhere, and you're not losing a stitch, you are simply elongating the garter stitch. As you become more familiar with the way it works, I'm sure other ways to use this stitch will come to mind.

Granite ridges

The raised rows of this pattern can serve a dual purpose—to insert a horizontal strip of color or to add a touch of texture. Add a knit stitch at each side edge for a seam allowance so, when sewing up the new color, lines will match at the seams. This stitch has a pleasant texture even when knit all in one color. Try it both ways.

Cast on an even number of stitches.
Rows 1, 3, and 5: Knit.
Rows 2 and 4: Purl.
Row 6: (You can change to a contrasting color for rows 6 and 7.) Knit 1 (edge stitch), *knit 2 together across row*, end with knit 1.
Row 7: Knit 1, *(knit 1, purl 1) into *each* stitch*, end with knit 1.
Row 8: Purl.

Rows 6 and 7 provide the contrast in texture and/or color. On row 6 you will be decreasing all along the row, and on row 7 you will be increasing all along the row. Instead of knitting every stitch on row 7, you are working a knit 1, purl 1 into every stitch. Turn your work to the back side and you will clearly see where the line is indented to form a ridge on the front.

Granite ridges knitted in two colors, above, and in a single color, below.

The slants

Create an oblique line in a garment with slants. They are worked with a minimum of fuss and can be knitted with as many colors as you please. Personally, I think they're less blatant when used with two colors, or as a texture contrast knitted with a smooth yarn. This is an easy stitch to learn. The zigzags are a combination of stockinette stitch and reverse stockinette stitch. They

may be slanted to the left or to the right. Actually, this gives the effect of bias knitting without increasing or decreasing at either side.

To slant the diagonal line to the right, maintain the same number of stitches throughout, and on every *right* side row move the group of reverse stockinette stitches one stitch to the right. To reverse the slant, move the group to the left. The group of reversed stockinette stitches may be as wide or as narrow as is appropriate for your design. The sweater below features 6 reverse stockinette stitches. The photo-

This V-neck pullover features diagonal bands of reverse stockinette stitch on front and back.

graph on page 84 shows a sweater with a slant of 7 stitches. The sweater on page 113 has an exaggerated stripe (about 20 stitches) only this time the stripe is knitted in stockinette stitch and the reversed stitch was used for the background. The fun part about knitting slants is that whenever you're tired of knitting in one direction you can change to another.

Florence's stitch

I don't know the name of this pattern stitch, but I like the way Florence used it in her glossy rayon cardigan. After knitting a sample, she decided that the back side of the stitch seemed to show off the lovely texture of the yarn better, and the right side of the stitch appeared too bulky for her petite figure. The design is a simple V-neck cardigan. What takes it a step beyond ordinary is the shiny rayon ribbon, the sparkly buttons, and low-key stitch. This is definitely a sweater to be worn for special occasions.

The rayon ribbon has a tendency to fray, and Florence told me she is especially careful to avoid sharp surfaces when she wears this sweater. The sweater is also very heavy. She knows that the weight of the yarn will cause it to creep eventually.

This stitch is made with two very different needle sizes used as a pair. Florence used size 10 and size 3 needles. Cast on an even number of stitches.

Row 1: Using the larger needle as the right-hand needle, knit 1 (edge stitch), *knit 1, yo*. Repeat between * *. End with knit 1 (edge stitch).

Row 2: Using the smaller needle as the right-hand needle, knit 1 (edge stitch), *slip the first 3 knit stitches onto the right-hand

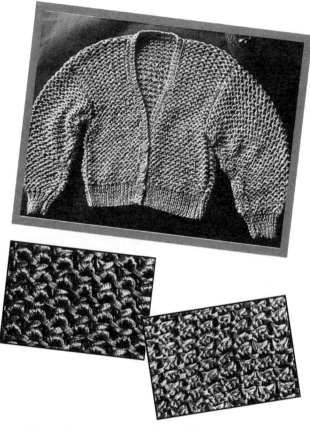

Florence's sweater was knitted from rayon ribbon. She decided to use the "wrong side" of her stitch (top inset) rather than the "right side" (bottom inset).

needle, letting the 3 yo's drop, then slip the stitches back to the left-hand needle and work them together—knitting, purling, then knitting*, repeat between *   *, knit 1 (edge stitch).

These two rows are worked throughout. Be sure to move the yarn to the back when knitting and move it to the front when purling.

Double cable

This is my version of the familiar cable stitch—two basic cables worked in opposite directions, divided by two stitches of reverse stockinette stitch, and offset by two reverse stockinette stitches on either side. I like to use this double cable as a center vertical line, and then divide it to make a border on either side of a classic V-neck sweater.

Work with an even number of stitches (I've used 14).

Rows 1, 3, 5, 7 (wrong side): Knit 2, purl 4, knit 2, purl 4, knit 2.

Row 2: Purl 2, slip the next 2 stitches to a cable holder or double-pointed needle, and hold in back, knit 2, knit 2 from holder, purl 2, slip next 2 stitches to holder and hold in front, knit 2, knit 2 from holder, purl 2.

Rows 4, 6, 8: Purl 2, knit 4, purl 2, knit 4, purl 2.

Repeat rows 1 through 8.

I like the effect of this double cable treatment so much it appears again in the sweater on page 120 as a horizontal hip band. A single cable band outlines the bateau neckline, too. It doesn't matter how the cable is used as long as it complements the overall design of your garment. It's fun to add small blocks of cable made with another color every now and then, and it won't distort your stitch gauge providing you've allocated plenty of room between cable blocks.

The sweater on page 66 features another version of the double cable which rises from a single stem. The sweater is merely four rectangles of garter stitch—but with a difference; one side is a soft camel color, the opposite side is off-white. It's completely reversible. Small diamond-shaped gussets

Double cable stitch.

The double cable divides to make a V-neck.

Entrelac knitted with contrasting colors.

were inserted at the underarm for comfort. The yarn is a lightweight wool and mohair, comparable in weight to knitting worsted.

Entrelac

Would you like to have some fun and do some mental and physical gymnastics at the same time? Try entrelac. Entrelac is the French word for interlace. When entrelac is worked in stockinette stitch, the effect looks like a garden trellis. When worked in garter stitch, it resembles a mosaic. It can also be knitted in a combination of both stitches. Entrelac is beautiful knitted all in one color, or with two or more colors. It's smashing in all white or cream because the high-low texture gives it a light and shadow appearance. This is also an effective way to combine a smooth yarn with a mohair or nubby yarn. For this technique, you'll have to go into hiding. It demands lots of concentration with no interruptions!

It all starts with a base of triangles which combine to form a rectangle. For this example, we'll start with 48 stitches to produce four triangles.

Cast on 48 stitches. *Purl 2, turn, knit these 2 stitches, turn, purl 3 (taking the last stitch from the left-hand needle), turn, knit 3, turn, purl 4, turn, knit 4. Continue this way until there are 12 stitches on the right-hand needle. Leave these stitches on a holder or double-pointed needle. Don't cut the yarn. Repeat from *, placing each triangle aside as completed, until there are four triangles.

You now have four triangles slanting to the right (looking at the right side of the knitting). Next you will make a left-slanting triangle to the right of the right-most triangle. Working into the last triangle, *knit 2, turn, purl 2, turn, increase 1 stitch in first stitch, skp (slip 1 stitch, knit next stitch, pass slip stitch over), turn, purl 3, turn, increase 1 stitch in the first knit stitch, knit 1, skp, turn, purl 4. Continue this way, working one extra stitch between the increase and decrease each time until all the stitches of the first triangle have been worked. Leave 12 stitches on a double-pointed needle.

*Pick up and knit 12 stitches along the left edge of the first triangle, turn, purl these stitches, turn, knit 11, skp (the slipped stitch is the end of the 12 stitches picked up, and the knit stitch is the first of the next triangle), turn, purl 12, turn, knit 11, skp, turn, purl 12. Continue like this until all the stitches of the next triangle are used up. Repeat from * twice more, picking up the 12 stitches along the left side of each of the next triangles.

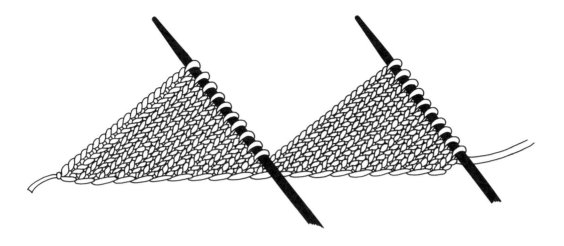

Step 1: Knit a series of four triangles, leaving the stitches on a double-pointed needle or stitch holder.

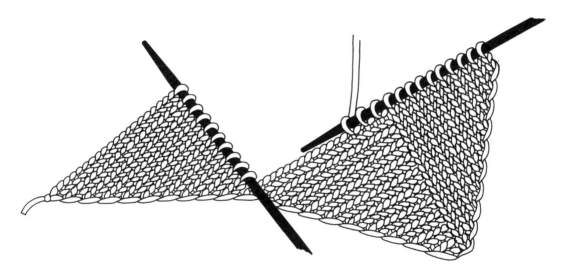

Step 2: Knit along the right edge of the last triangle.

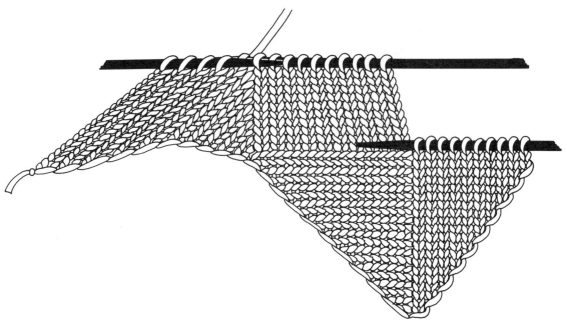

*Step 3: Pick up and knit along the left edge of
each triangle, forming rectangles.*

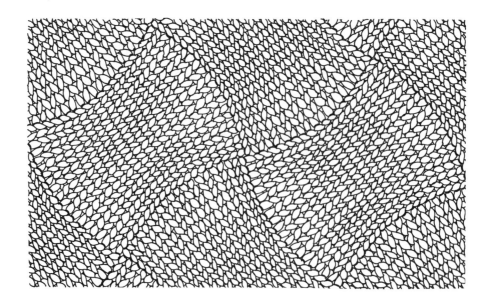

Completed entrelac.

When this is completed, pick up and knit 12 stitches along the left edge of the last triangle, turn, purl 2 together, purl 10, turn, knit 11, turn, purl 2 together, purl 9, turn, knit 10, turn. Continue this way until 1 stitch is left. Pick up and purl 11 stitches along the straight edge of the just-completed triangle, turn, *knit 12, turn, purl 11, purl 2 together (use the last stitch of the 12 stitches picked up and the first stitch from the next rectangle), turn, knit 12, turn, purl 11, purl 2 together, turn. Continue until all the stitches have been used. Pick up and purl 12 stitches along the side of the next rectangle. Repeat from * 3 times.

Repeat this whole procedure for as many lines of rectangles as necessary. To finish off a rectangular section, **pick up and purl 11 stitches along the side of the last triangle, turn, knit 12, turn, purl 2 together, purl 9, purl 2 together (use the last stitch on the needle and the first stitch of the following rectangle), turn, knit 11, turn, purl 2 together, purl 8, purl 2 together, turn, knit 10, turn. Continue this way until one stitch is left. Repeat from ** 3 more times. Fasten off.

To finish the entrelacs, you will work another row of triangles. These fill out the open spaces left by the final row of rectangles.

When I first experimented with entrelac, I nearly went bananas, but as I became familiar with sequences of picking up stitches and connecting them, it began to form a rhythm. You could ask a family member or a friend to read the steps to you while your hands are doing the gymnastics with the needles and yarn.

Knitting up one side and down the other of the triangles forms interlaced rectangles, and it looks gorgeous. Make the entrelacs with any number of stitches. Try a sample with two colors; the result looks as though you've woven one color through the other. Entrelac is a marvelous way to use up all those bits and pieces of yarn left over from other projects—just add a different yarn each time you knit another rectangle.

And here's a sneaky way to achieve a similar effect. Knit up a bunch of rectangles all the same size, and sew them together in opposite directions to simulate the trellis. Fill in the jagged edges all around the perimeter with triangles. The real entrelac, of course, looks much more professional, but if the pieces are sewn together carefully, the result is almost as good. Try a few for the experience.

Swirls

A swirl is a hexagon made by knitting a series of six connected triangles. They may be made with one color or many colors. Make several and appliqué them to a basic sweater. A single swirl may be used as an interesting pocket.

Work with an uneven number of stitches. For your sample, start with 15 stitches. This is the base of the first triangle. Knit one row. Decrease 1 stitch at the beginning and end of the next row, and on *every other* row until 3 stitches remain. Knit these 3 stitches together. There is now one stitch on the right-hand needle. Working so that the left edge of the triangle is facing you, pick up 14 stitches along that edge. Knit one row. Work the remaining part of the triangle as just described. Continue this way until six triangles have been worked. Fasten off, leaving a generous length of yarn. Thread a

Swirls.

tapestry needle onto the yarn and weave the edge of the last triangle to the free edge of the first triangle.

The swirls may be knitted from garter or stockinette stitch, although I think you'll like the garter stitch better because the edges will not curl. A duplicate stitch worked in a contrasting color over the connecting edges of the triangles gives an interesting touch. Stitch them to the sweater fabric with a tiny overcast stitch.

Houndstooth check

Have you wanted to attempt a jacquard or two-color motif but been afraid to? Here are some easy ones for starters. The check is suitable as an all-over pattern, providing the stitch is to be the focal point of your design. Or use it as a border somewhere on your garment. This is another way to enhance the stockinette stitch with snippets of color. For practice, try it first with two colors of a smooth yarn, then with two yarns of different textures. Use a fine mohair with a flat background for texture that doesn't detract from the pattern. Keep a record of the results. This check has 4 stitches to a group, so we'll start with 20 stitches.

Row 1: *Knit 2 main color, 2 contrasting color*.
Row 2: Purl 1 with main color, *2 contrasting color, 2 main color*. End with 2 contrasting color, 1 main color.
Row 3: Knit 1 contrasting color, *2 main color, 2 contrasting color*, end with 2 main color, 1 contrasting color.
Row 4: *Purl 2 contrasting color, 2 main color*.

Work these four rows for a complete color sequence. One ball of yarn is necessary for each color. For this small-scale pattern, the yarn not in use is passed *behind* the stitches being worked on knit rows and in *front* on purl rows. The fabric is quite firm.

Slipstitch houndstooth check

This version changes color every two rows instead of changing color within each row. The slipped stitches pull the contrasting color up into the following row. Because the colors are changed every two rows, it isn't necessary to carry them across each row. There are 3 stitches in each check, so

Row 1: *Knit 2 main color, 2 contrasting color*.
Row 2: *Purl 2 contrasting color, 2 main color*.
Row 3: *Knit 2 contrasting color, 2 main color*.
Row 4: *Purl 2 main color, 2 contrasting color*.

There are hundreds more color pattern stitches to try, but as an introduction to two-color knitting, these should keep you busy for a while. And don't forget to check the opposite side of these pattern stitches—you may like that side even better!

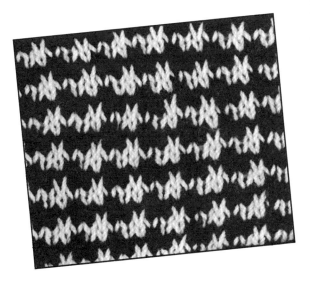

Slipstitch houndstooth check.

cast on any number that is divisible by 3. For your sample, start with 18 stitches.
Row 1: With main color, knit 1, *slip 1 as if to purl, knit 2*.
Row 2: With main color, purl.
Row 3: With contrasting color, knit 1, *knit 2, slip 1 as if to purl*.
Row 4: With contrasting color, purl.

Checked stockinette stitch

This checked stitch, also knitted with two colors, shows an even distribution of the alternate colors. Worked in blocks throughout a sweater, it offers an interesting contrast of pattern. There are 4 stitches to a group, so cast on any number of stitches divisible by 4.

Checked stockinette stitch.

This sweater features cable around the neckline and sleeves. The abstract design was done with slipstitch crochet.

Double cable runs up the center of both sides of this reversible sweater knitted in wool and mohair. Note the small, diamond-shaped gussets under the the arms.

Chapter 8
ADDED TOUCHES

Look at your knit as a painter's canvas, then turn that canvas into your very own signature knit. You can do it in many ways—by adding pockets in unconventional places, by smocking down the side or across a yoke, or by slipstitch crocheting along the surface. Duplicate stitch and other embroidery stitches will liven up the plainest sweater. You can also paint a design directly onto the surface of the knitted material. And then there are appliqués, such as animals, flowers, or initials, that may be knitted or made from scraps of woven material. Tassels, pompons, and fringe in matching or contrasting yarn can decorate necklines, sleeves, or hems. And when you tire of these decorations, you can easily remove them or switch them around.

A dash of interesting pattern stitch inserted in surprising places might be another special touch. Think about curved or angled hems, or slanted pockets. How about beading or sequins to transform your classic design into evening wear? A row of crocheted gold or silver trim immediately adds elegance to the plainest sweater or jacket. Outline a pocket with metallic thread or work a more intricate design onto the surface of the knitted material.

Rather than knitting special touches into a garment, I frequently work them onto the surface because surface decorations are easily removed when I feel like changing the design. It's simpler to change the surface than to unravel the sweater. Mary, one of the group members, commented that because she had invested so much time and energy in creating the design below, she'd never even think of unraveling. And I don't blame her; however, for a change, she could add a little removable glitz to the flower by outlining it with gold thread or filling it in with beads or sequins.

The hazard of knitting design features *into* a garment is that they can date your

The stylized flower on Mary's pullover could be enhanced with metallic yarn or sequins.

garment long before it's ever worn out. That doesn't mean that your knits need be dull. With smidges of color, touches of texture, and smart shaping, your handknits will be chic and fashionable for many years.

Smocking

Smocking is a lovely way to decorate a handknit. The background is formed by making vertical rows of knit stitches on a purl background, and then joining these rows at staggered intervals with hand stitching. Smocking will reduce the width of the material by a couple of inches. To accommodate this change, either use a larger size needle for the smocked section, or add some extra stitches on the row preceding the smocked section. Work this out on a sample swatch before trying it on your sweater or jacket. For example, the sweater on page 111 was knitted with purl 4, knit 1 as the background. Rather than increase the number of stitches for the yoke, I used a needle one size larger than the one used for the body of the sweater. Changing the stitch gauge in this way provided just enough additional width to compensate for the width lost through smocking.

To do smocking, use a blunt-point tapestry needle threaded with thread or yarn. Go under the first *knit* stitch and come up from behind the second knit stitch on the left and over those same stitches. Do this twice. You have pulled the knit stitches together with the horizontal sewing stitch. From the back again, come up to the left of the next two knit stitches, and repeat as just described. Work this way across the row. With a purl 4, knit 1 background, you will be pulling groups of six stitches together, the four

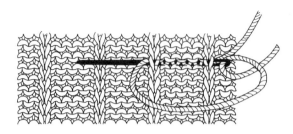

Step 1: Go under the first knit stitch and up from behind the second knit stitch, two times.

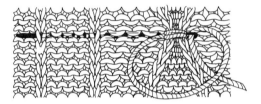

Step 2: From the back, come up to the left of the next two knit stitches and repeat step 1.

The second row of smocking is started one stitch over to give the characteristic diamond pattern.

purl stitches and a knit stitch on either end.

Start the second row of smocking one line of knit stitches over and four, five, or six rows up (depending on how wide apart you prefer the smocking). If you're a stickler about precision, you may want the last row of stitching to match the first. I've never been too concerned about that. What I try to do is make sure that the smocking meets at the shoulder line.

It isn't necessary to be skilled with needle and thread to produce smocking. However, please do experiment on a sample swatch until you feel confident. I usually use purl 4, knit 1 as background, but you may want to vary the number of in-between stitches.

The sweaters below and on page 66 illustrate different ways to achieve interesting designs with slipstitch crochet. If you see a design that looks as if it might be appropriate, adapt it; or make up designs just to test your creative powers. If you are worried about maintaining a straight line, run a contrasting thread through the knitting as a guide, then follow that thread. Be sure to remove the guiding thread after you're done.

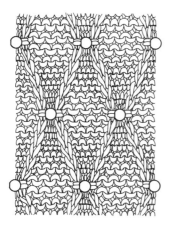

Beads can be added to smocking on the tops of the horizontal stitches.

Slipstitch crochet

Slipstitch crochet is a wonderfully flexible way to decorate the surface of your knitting. You can go any direction you want— straight, diagonally, or around in circles.

Slipstitch crochet can be used to achieve interesting designs on otherwise plain sweaters. And the designs can be removed or changed later for a different look.

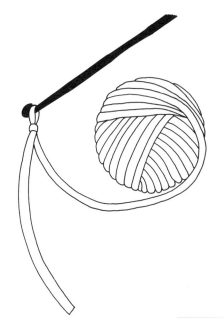

Step 1: Make a slip knot and put it on your crochet hook.

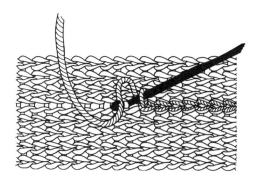

Step 2: Slide the hook under the horizontal thread of the knitted stitch and catch the yarn to be crocheted.

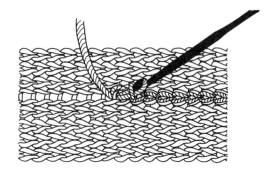

Step 3: Pull the crochet yarn under the horizontal thread and up through the loop on the hook.

With a medium-size crochet hook, make a slip knot 3 or 4 inches from the end of the yarn to be crocheted. Slide your crochet hook through the loop. Place your other hand underneath the material (this helps to keep the material from slipping around). With the first loop on the hook, slide the hook underneath the horizontal thread of the first stitch, catch the yarn and pull it underneath that horizontal thread and up through the loop on the hook. Continue this way, always catching the yarn underneath the horizontal thread of the next stitch. Work until you have completed your design. The fun part of slipstitch surface decorating is that it is easily removed. A word of caution—use a yarn compatible with the sweater yarn to avoid laundering problems.

Duplicate stitch

Duplicate stitching covers already-knitted stitches by following their path with contrasting yarn. Duplicate stitching may be

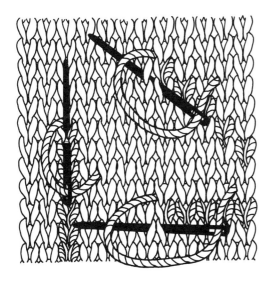

Above, duplicate stitching can be done vertically, horizontally, or diagonally.
Below, an argyle pattern for duplicate stitching.

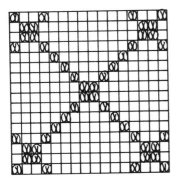

used just as you would slipstitch crochet, and in any direction.

Practice on a swatch of knitted material. Thread your tapestry needle with some yarn in a contrasting color so the stitches can be easily checked. Starting from the back side of your swatch, insert the point of the needle into the base of a stitch. Leave a 5- or 6-inch tail of yarn. Bring the needle to the front of your work, with the yarn lying over to the right side. Now slip the needle under the two loops at the top of the same stitch. Pull the yarn through. Try to match the tension of the new stitch to that of the already-knitted stitch. Push the needle through to the wrong side at the base of the first stitch, and out at the base of the next stitch to be worked.

Try the duplicate stitch vertically for starters, then work a few stitches horizontally or diagonally. It's best to start from the top and work down because working from bottom to top could pull the yarn awkwardly into the next stitch and may not cover it properly. But that's not a rule fixed in concrete. If it's easier to work in one direction than another, go ahead. When working diagonally, you will be working one row up and one row to the right or left, depending on your design. Adjust the tension as you stitch, if necessary, to avoid puckering the material. This procedure takes some practice and patience.

The duplicate stitch is a wonderful technique not only for decorating, but for hiding mistakes. But don't overdo it, because too much extra weight of one yarn on top of another might eventually cause the material to stretch.

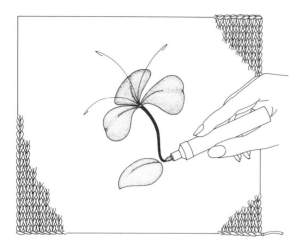

Paint your sweaters with special textile pens designed for this purpose. The possibilities are endless.

Painting your sweater

When I discovered textile pens for writing or painting on all types of fabric, a whole new world of surface decorating presented itself. These pens are easy to use, and the ink is permanent so it can be machine washed or dry cleaned. Before you commit yourself to a painted surface design, be absolutely sure about what you intend to do. After the design has been applied to the fabric, let the ink dry, then set it with an iron. The manufacturer suggests setting the ink in your clothes dryer, but I wouldn't take any chances with knits—use an iron. Keep the pens out of reach of little ones or you may end up with some permanent artwork on your walls.

Fringing

You can convert a rather ordinary garment into a snazzy one by adding fringe. Fringes are also easily removed when the mood has passed. Add a double fringe as a border along the bottom of a sweater, decorate a simple sleeve, or touch up a neckline with a dash of fringe. Make it from the same or contrasting yarn, but be sure it's compatible with the sweater yarn. Make your fringe any length or thickness. A single strand of yarn makes a two-strand fringe, so decide on the thickness and spacing before you cut the yarn.

Let's look at the procedure for making a four-strand fringe. Cut a piece of firm cardboard about 2 inches wide and 3½ inches long. For each group of four strands, wrap the yarn around the cardboard twice. For an edging with 33 fringes, for example, wrap the yarn 66 times. Cut the yarn across the bottom of the cardboard. To attach the fringe, hold two strands together and fold them in half. With the right side of the garment facing you, put your crochet hook through the stitch where you intend to connect the fringe. Catch both strands with the

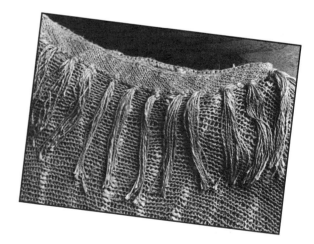

Fringes can be any length, in matching or contrasting yarn.

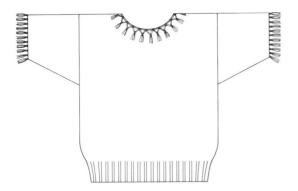

Create a new look by adding fringe at the neckline or on the sleeves of a sweater.

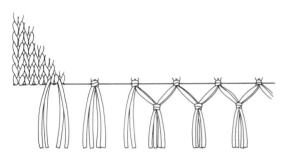

After the fringes are attached to the sweater, several strands from adjacent fringe groups can be knotted together.

hook and pull them through halfway. This makes a large loop. Now pull the ends of the yarn through the loop; one group of fringe has been fastened. Make one fringe in every other stitch. After you have attached all the fringes, give each one a little pull to anchor the yarn. If the edges look a little ragged, trim them with your scissors. Hint: After laundering a fringed sweater, straighten out the strands with your fingers while the sweater is still damp.

Pockets

Put in unusual places, pockets can add interest where least expected. Pockets may be knitted right into the material (insert pockets), or they can be knitted separately and sewed on (patch pockets). The sweater below shows patch pockets sewn to the front and back of the sweater, and on one sleeve as well. The pockets are positioned to merge with lines of the material so as not to disturb the established stripes. The front and back are different, so the sweater may be worn either way.

This hip-length sweater with dolman sleeves features patch pockets on the front, the back, and one sleeve. The pockets were carefully aligned to match the stripes on the sweater.

74

Patch, or stitched-on pockets are the easiest to make and to apply. They can be any depth and width you please and can be applied anywhere. After a pocket is knitted, pin, then baste it to your sweater. Use a ruler to line up pockets if you intend for them to be parallel. With matching or blending yarn, taking small stitches, overcast the pocket to the body of the sweater around three edges, leaving the top open. Try to maintain the same tension as the knitted stitches to prevent pulling. When carefully done, the overcast stitches will be almost invisible.

Another version of a patch pocket features a knitted facing on all four sides. To knit the pocket, cast on the necessary number of stitches, less four. Purl one row. Knit the next row, increasing in the first and last stitches. Purl back. Knit the next row in back of every stitch (turning row). Purl back. On the next row, increase one stitch in the first stitch, knit 2 stitches, slip the next stitch as if to purl; knit across the row to the last 3 stitches, slip one stitch as if to purl, knit 2 stitches, increase one stitch in the last stitch. Purl back. Knit one more row, increasing in the first and last stitches. Work even until the pocket is the desired depth, slipping the third stitch from each end of the rows. When the pocket is the correct depth, work in reverse, decreasing instead of increasing. The vertical slipped stitches form the side facings and the stitches knitted in back form the top and bottom facings. Fold these four edges to the wrong side and lightly slipstitch them in place with matching yarn. Pin, then overcast the pocket to the body of sweater.

Insert pockets are neat and unobtrusive but they are more complicated than patch pockets. Conventional insert pockets are

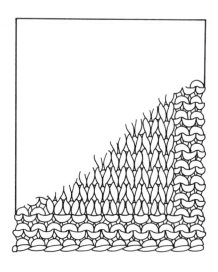

Above, a simple patch pocket in stockinette stitch with decorative garter stitch border.

Below, a patch pocket with knitted facings on all four sides.

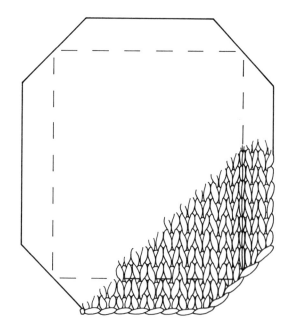

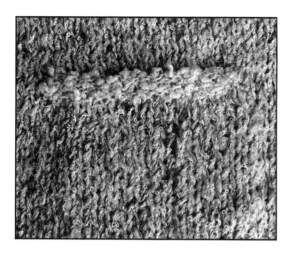

Horizontal insert pocket with contrasting trim.

The sweater jacket below has vertical insert pockets.

usually horizontal. Slope them to the right or left, or insert them vertically for an interesting effect. They're most easily knitted directly into the garment, which requires advance planning.

To knit a horizontal insert pocket, decide how deep and wide your pocket should be and determine the number of stitches involved according to your stitch gauge. With stockinette stitch, knit the pocket first, and, ending on a purl row, leave those stitches on a holder. (No matter what stitch you use for the sweater, make the pocket linings from stockinette stitch because it is less bulky.) Knit the body of the garment until you reach the desired depth to accommodate the depth of the pocket lining. This time, end on the *right* side of the material. Knit over to the space set aside for the pocket, then bind off the same number of stitches as on the holder. Finish the row. On the next row, work over to the bound-off stitches. The right side of the stitches on the holder should face the inside of the garment. Knit the stitches from the holder and complete the row. When the body of the sweater is completed, you may want to add a border at the top edge of the pocket. Work a couple of rows of single crochet over the bound-off stitches for a neat edge.

You can make a narrow facing by picking up stitches with a size smaller needle, from the right side through the bound-off stitches of the pocket opening. Knit four or five rows of stockinette stitch. Bind off. Turn the facing to the inside, and neatly slipstitch to the inside of the pocket—not the lining. Turn the sweater to the wrong side and pin, carefully slipstitch the three sides of the lining to the body of the sweater. Try to maintain the same tension as the knitted stitches. Very lightly steam the linings.

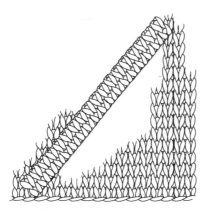

Right-sloping insert pocket. For a firm no-stretch edge, knit a separate band and back-stitch it to the pocket opening.

Insert pockets are best when knitted right into the garment.

To slope an insert pocket to the right, knit over to the place designated for the base of the slope. Slip the stitches on the left needle to a holder. On the stitches remaining on the right needle, work two rows even, then decrease one stitch every row on the left edge until the opening is as large as you've planned. Slip the remaining stitches to a holder. Make the lining or underpocket by casting on the number of stitches decreased for the slant. Knit even for about 1½ inches. Slip the first set of stitches from the holder back on to the needle to the left of those stitches. Knit across all the stitches and continue to work even until the work reaches the depth of the stitches on the right-hand needle. Work across all the stitches including those on the right-hand needle and continue working your garment.

To finish off the slanted pocket, knit a separate ribbed band. Connect it to the

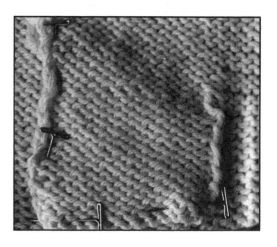

Turn the garment over and overcast the free edges of the pocket to the sweater.

slanted pocket by putting the right sides together and backstitching the two edges together. Tuck in the ends and stitch. Turn the sweater to wrong side, pin, and overcast the free edges to the body of sweater. Lightly steam. To slope the pocket to the left, simply reverse the steps as described.

Necklines

To make the popular bateau or boat neckline, no shaping is necessary. Simply bind off straight across when the sweater is the proper length from shoulder to hem. Leave an opening large enough for your head to slip through comfortably, and sew the shoulder seams to that point. Make an inside facing by picking up stitches all around the neck edge; knit even in stockinette stitch for about 3/4 inch. Bind off loosely. Use a size larger needle if you're inclined to bind off tightly. Turn the facing to the inside and slipstitch it in place.

To shape the front of the neck opening for a crew neckline, knit up to the base of the neck—about to the hollow between your collar bones. Divide the stitches into three even parts and slip the center group of stitches onto a stitch holder. These are the base of the crew neck. The remaining stitches on each side of the reserved center stitches form the neckline up to the shoulders. Working both sides at the same time, decrease one stitch on each side every other row a couple of times, to round out the neckline. Work even for the desired length—usually about 3 inches. Bind off.

The back of the neckline may also be shaped, but I rarely find it necessary. If you do prefer a bit of shaping, work until the back measures a couple of inches more

The crew neck was folded to the outside and stitched rather than to the inside.

than the front neck base. Divide the stitches into three groups, reserve the center third for the base, then decrease a couple of times every other row at each neck edge. Bind off.

To make the band, you can sew the shoulder seams together and pick up stitches all around the neckline with a circular needle or three double-pointed needles, sliding the stitches on holders onto your needle as you come to them. Or leave one shoulder seam free and pick up stitches starting at the right shoulder facing you. Knit the stitches from the front holder; pick up the stitches all around the edge. Knit the stitches from the back holder; pick up the remaining stitches. Work in knit 1, purl 1 ribbing (or any other stitch that will complement your design) for about 2 inches. Fold the band in half to the inside and slipstitch in place. Bind off loosely in pattern.

For a deeper scooped neckline, work as before, but start the neck opening 2 or 3 inches lower than the crew neckline. All other steps are the same.

And, of course, there's the classic V-neckline. The traditional V-neck is usually started about the same row as the space set aside for the start of the underarm. If your armhole will start 10 inches down from the shoulder, start the V shaping on that row, too. This is just a guideline; you can start the V anywhere you please. Some sweaters feature a very deep V—almost to the waistline.

"How do I know how many times to decrease for a well-fitting V-neck?" you might ask. Decide how many stitches will be necessary for the back of the neck, because the stitches to be decreased will equal that number. For instance, if there are 40 stitches across the back of the neck, then it will be necessary to decrease 20 stitches at each side of the V. Place a marker at the center of the row where you plan to begin the V. As a general rule, decreases should end about 3/4 inch below the top of the shoulder. Figure how many rows there will be from the marker to the shoulder by multiplying the neckline depth by the number of rows per inch. Then subtract 3/4 inch. This is one instance where counting rows is important. To determine how often to decrease, divide that number of rows by the number of necessary decreases. For example, a measurement of 40 rows, divided by 20 (number of decreases), shows that you should decrease every second row 20 times. Work both sides of the V at the same time using two balls of yarn to be sure all the decreases are done on the same row.

Often the numbers will not work out evenly. If that's the case, alternate decreases by working them every second row and every fourth row at the lower end of the neckline, then switching to every second row closer to the shoulder.

This classic V-neck pullover was made from double strands of slubbed cotton and trimmed with stripes of silk. The neckline is outlined with a single row of slipstitch crochet.

Make a neckband by picking up stitches around the neckline, or make a separate band and sew it on later. I'm rarely ecstatic about picking up stitches for the neckband; I think it's easier to hide an irregular edge by sewing the band over the edge. But you decide what works best for you.

To make a well-fitting V-neckband, measure the number of inches along each side of the V and across the back of the neck. Multiply this number by the number of stitches in your gauge. For a measurement of 26 inches, for example, with a stitch gauge of 5 stitches per inch, you will need 130 stitches. With circular or double-pointed needles one or two sizes smaller than that used for the body, cast on 130 stitches, plus one. The extra stitch is a slipped stitch at the base of the V. Place markers on either side of that stitch. Working in ribbing or whatever stitch you choose, decrease one stitch before the marker, slip the center stitch, decrease one stitch. Work these decreases on *every* row until the band is the desired width. On the right side of your work, knit in the back of every stitch (turning row). Continuing in the original stitch, increase instead of decrease on each side of the center slipped stitch, until the band is the same depth as on the decreased side. Bind off loosely in pattern. The same procedure can be used to make a neckband for the scoop or crew neck, but eliminate the center slipped stitch.

After the shoulder seams have been sewn together, pin the neckband to the sweater, being careful to place the center stitch at the point where the V begins. Baste the neckband in place, easing it in if necessary. With matching yarn, overcast one edge of the band to the sweater with tiny stitches. Fold the band to the inside and slipstitch the other edge. Try to maintain the same tension as the knitted material.

Above, a vest with a deep V-neck is stylish for both men and women.
Below, Muriel's mohair vest.

Collars and turtlenecks

Turtlenecks are pretty easy to plan. Usually started from a crew neck base, the turtleneck collar may be made separately and sewn on, or you can pick up stitches and work from there.

To make the picked-up version, work a row of single crochet all around the neck edge to even up any irregular stitches. With a smaller size circular needle, pick up stitches all around the neck edge. Work even in ribbing until the collar is a comfortable depth—6 or 7 inches is usually enough. Bind off loosely in pattern; this is necessary for the turtleneck to retain elasticity.

For an exaggerated version that falls into a cowl, work even for 2 or 3 inches. Decrease 10 or 12 stitches (assuming you're using a worsted-weight yarn), evenly spaced on one row. Knit another 3 or 4 rows, again decrease 8 or 10 stitches evenly spaced. Work even for an inch or so, then increase 10 stitches evenly spaced, every 3 or 4 rows, until the collar is wide enough to drape softly. You'll have to decide how much or how little is comfortable for you. Turtlenecks can use up a fair bit of yarn, so be sure you have enough.

The method for making a separate turtleneck to be sewn on requires the same procedure as the picked-up version, but I think it offers a neater connection around the neckline. Knit the sewn-on turtleneck with either circular or straight needles.

With straight needles there will be a seam where the two sides meet. Position this seam at one shoulder seam when you sew the turtleneck onto the sweater. To sew the turtleneck on, pin it to the right side of the neck edge with the seam on the outside, easing in any loose stitches on the neck edge as you work. With matching or blending yarn and your blunt-point tapestry needle, backstitch the two edges together. The backstitches should be worked just underneath the edge stitches so that the loops are not visible on the right side. The smaller the stitches, the neater the seam. Watch the tension or the stitches might pop as you slip the garment over your head.

Add a collar to a classic crew neck and you've instantly changed the design. For a

A twisted rib turtleneck embellishes this pullover knitted in broad ribbed sections alternated with sections of twisted stockinette stitch.

double-faced collar, measure the circumference of the neckline—stretch it out a bit so your head can slip through—and cast on the appropriate number of stitches on straight needles according to your stitch gauge. Knitting back and forth, work even for a couple of inches. On the next right-side row, increase one stitch in the first stitch, work across the row, and increase one stitch in the last stitch. Repeat these increases every *fourth* row twice more, or until the collar is the desired depth. Work four more rows even, ending on the wrong side. On the next right-side row, work across the row, knitting in the back of every stitch (turning row). Work four rows, then reverse the procedure, decreasing instead of increasing. Knit four more rows. This allows for about 1/2 inch to 3/4 inch of material for the fold-back at the neck edge. Bind off loosely. Fold the piece in half with right sides facing each other and sew the two short ends together with tiny backstitches. Turn the collar back to the right side. With one right-side edge of the collar facing the right-side edge of the garment, pin the two edges together, then backstitch with matching yarn. Fold the free edge over to the inside of the neck edge and over the sewn seam and lightly slipstitch. This collar can be worn flat or as a stand-up collar. Use a simple pattern stitch to give it an interesting texture, then add a bit of the same stitch somewhere else on the sweater.

When planning a collar for a front-buttoned garment, reduce the number of stitches by an inch or two to allow for the opening. (This isn't necessary for a zippered closure.)

And how about an Oriental collar? This tiny stand-up collar is the easiest of all. Make this collar by picking up stitches

A stand-up collar, curved hem, and raglan kimono sleeves give this sweater Oriental flair.

around the neck edge, or make it separately and sew it on. Measure the neck opening as usual. With needles a size smaller than those used for the body of the sweater, cast on the required number of stitches according to the stitch gauge. Work even for 1½ to 2 inches. Knit a turning row, then work even until the section after the turning row measures about 1/4 inch less than the first section. Bind off. Fold the collar at the turning row with right sides facing and pin, then sew the two short ends together. Turn it back to the right side and pin, then stitch one edge to the neck edge in the same manner described for the other collar designs. Baste the free edge to the inside of the neck edge, just covering the seam.

This handspun wool sweater features a stand-up collar with braided ties. It was knitted in garter stitch with insets of stockinette and reverse stockinette in sleeves, pockets, and yoke. The matching four-panel skirt was knitted in garter stitch with a hem of reverse and plain stockinette stitch.

To prevent this stand-up collar from rolling over, you may want to insert interfacing made from pellon, a piece of muslin, or any other rather firm fabric. After the sweater has been blocked, including the collar, cut a piece of interfacing just a tad smaller than the width and depth of the collar. Remove the basting stitches and slide the interfacing between the fold. Pin, then slipstitch the free edge of the collar to the inside of the neckline. It's that simple.

A bit of embroidery might be an interesting addition if it works with the rest of the design. And this collar is a natural for setting off a lovely silk ascot or a piece of interesting jewelry.

Buttonholes

I think buttonholes are the pits, so with the exception of cardigans, most of my designs are planned without buttonholes. Occasionally I'll include a simple eyelet when a shoulder opening is part of the design. Sometimes I'll fake it and add a button even when there's no buttonhole simply because I think a gorgeous button will enhance the design. But the time will come when you want to make a cardigan or jacket, so you may as well add a couple of buttonholes to your knitting skills.

Decide early on where to place the buttonhole so there won't be any surprises. When I'm working with a bulky yarn and large needles, the eyelet is usually fine for an average-size button. To make an eyelet buttonhole, yarn-over, then knit 2 stitches together. On the next row, work straight across, including the yarn-over. That's all there is to it. The eyelet buttonhole needs no further finishing.

When making buttonholes for a cardigan, make a note of the center front length, from the center of the neckline to the bottom of the sweater, then decide on the size of the buttonhole. Some knitters choose the buttons when they buy the yarn, others choose them after the sweater is sewn together. It is important that the button fit the buttonhole and that the buttonholes are evenly spaced and do not allow gapping. For a sweater knitted from bulky yarn, buttonholes can be about 4½ inches apart. For medium- or worsted-weight yarns, 3 to 4 inches apart is a good rule of thumb. On a basic cardigan, plan the first buttonhole about 1/2 inch below the neckline, and the last about the same distance from the bottom of the sweater. For example, if the measurement from the neckline to the bottom of the sweater is 18 inches, subtract 1/2 inch at the top and bottom to get 17 inches. If the buttons are to be spaced 3 inches apart, divide 17 by 3 to get 5 buttonholes every 3¼ to 3½ inches.

It's best to work both sides of the cardigan at the same time. On each row that you work in a buttonhole, knit in a short piece of a contrasting color yarn on the side where you plan to sew on the button. After the button is sewn, just remove the extra yarn. This way the button will be placed exactly right.

To make a horizontal hole, measure your button, then bind off the required number of stitches to fit the button. Finish the row. On the next row, knit up to within one stitch of the bound-off stitches, increase one stitch in the next stitch, then cast on one stitch *less* than the bound-off number. Finish the row. It's not a perfect buttonhole, but it's pretty good. If there's a loose stitch at either or both corners, correct it by working around the opening with buttonhole stitch. If your yarn is too bulky for this finish, use regular buttonhole twist. As a matter of fact, I prefer to use the firmer buttonhole twist around buttonholes that will be used a lot, especially on children's sweaters. It's much more substantial than yarn, which can become frayed with constant use.

Some experts recommend making buttonholes with the sewing machine after the sweater is done. If you never intend to unravel your sweater, I guess the sewing machine could be one answer. However, many times I've resorted to the sewing machine and regretted it later, because unraveling the garment was then out of the question. I have a beautiful Irish knit that was made years ago from a very special hard-finish, water-repellent Swedish rug yarn. Although the sweater is about twenty years old, the yarn is still beautiful but the shape is hopelessly outdated. I've hesitated to unravel it because I foolishly had the buttonholes cut after the sweater was completed. Of course there probably would be plenty of reusable yarn from the back and sleeves, but I wouldn't be able to recover all of it. That project is still on my "maybe" list.

You can also knit the sweater without knitting in the buttonholes, then add crocheted loops later. Personally, I don't think crocheted buttonholes are very neat-looking.

To buttonhole or not to buttonhole—try them out and make up your own mind. But don't stew over them. You can always use ties or zippers or avoid closures altogether.

Ruffles

Add an applied ruffle down the front of your sweater or diagonally from shoulder to hem, or put ruffles around the sleeves. To avoid laundering problems, make the ruffle from the same type of yarn as the rest of the sweater.

Cast on the number of stitches required to make the ruffle the necessary length. Knit one row. On the next row, increase one stitch in *every* stitch. Work even until the ruffle is the desired width. Work in garter, stockinette, or a pattern stitch for added texture. Bind off.

To attach the ruffle, pin it to the sweater, easing in if necessary. If you are not sure you can keep the ruffle in a straight line, thread a tapestry needle with a contrasting color and run the yarn through the stitches on the sweater in a straight line. This will give you a guide for lining up the ruffle. Neatly overcast the narrow edge of the ruffle to the sweater. Pull any loose ends to the inside and weave them in.

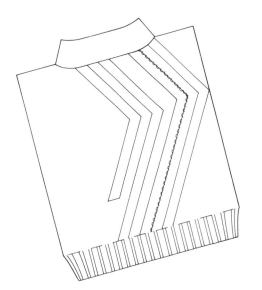

This striking red and white sweater can be worn with either side as the front. The dropped waistline and diagonal striping provide the illusion of elongating the figure.

Chapter 9
CONNECTING THE PARTS

I know knitters who love to work with beautiful yarns. And they find creating the design fun. But oh, how they dread connecting all the pieces! In my opinion, those connections can spell the difference between a well-made garment with a professional appearance that will endure through years of wear, and one that can fall apart after being worn only a few times. Sloppy connections can spoil the whole design.

At a recent convention, a highly regarded person in the fashion world asked me how I had the nerve to wear a store-bought sweater. I happened to be wearing the sweater on page 47. When I asked her what gave her that idea, she pointed out that the seams looked too perfect to have been done by hand. I could have kissed her! I showed her how I had sewn the seams in backstitch with matching yarn. Actually, it was a left-handed compliment, but she made my day! That sweater is fifteen years old, and the seams are still as sturdy and true as the day they were sewn.

The French are masters at beautiful seaming. After carefully scrutinizing their methods, I decided ages ago that no matter what I knitted, I would pay as much attention to the connections as to the design and knitting—regardless of how much time it

took. You may have to psych yourself up when it comes to this final step, but, believe me, when you've accomplished a beautiful seam and all the parts fall into place, you'll be glad you've taken the time to hone your skills.

This is the part of knitting that many members of the group wished would disappear, so I suggested they use the time to listen to music or begin planning their next great design. That's what I do—think ahead, so by the time everything is all connected, I've thought out my next design.

Seams

Most instructions advise pressing all the parts before sewing them together. I thoroughly disagree with this because there's so much danger of distorting the pieces. My motto is sew first, then press as necessary, and I've stuck to it for as long as I can remember. You ask, "What about all those curled edges? How do you keep them flat?" When the edges are carefully pinned and basted, you shouldn't have any trouble. Place your T-pins close together, then baste. As you baste, shove the curled edge up with your finger. That's why I recommend including one or two knit stitches in addition to the correct number of stitches at the beginning and end of every row to form a small seam allowance. This extra seam allowance is not too bulky and will lie flat when blocked. Sometimes, I've purposely added a conventional 5/8-inch seam allowance, so that bit of extra material was there if I needed it . . . and I have.

Don't sew the seams only to find out later that things don't match up. Try on your garment after basting. How does it feel? Do the shoulders match? Does the neckline rest where it's supposed to? How about stripes or pattern stitches? Do they meet at the seams the way you planned? What about those edge stitches? Do they need easing in? Check all of these areas, and anything else that might need attention before making a permanent connection.

If all is well, sew the shoulder seams first, making sure that any bound-off stitches don't creep through to the right side. Should one piece be a smidge wider than the other, ease the material in between the pins before you baste and sew. Add a touch of light steam and the easing will never be noticeable. Next, sew the sleeve to the armhole, then the sleeve and side seams in one long seam. Check again for loose edge stitches. These, too should be eased gently into the seam as you sew. Other parts, such as facings, neckbands, and pockets, may be sewn on later. By the way, as you sew, leave a generous tail of yarn at the beginning and end of each seam in case it's necessary later to remove the stitching. I call these my "traffic signs," and they are a most welcome assist when knitted garments need to be altered for some reason.

Machine sewing is successful only with lighter weight smooth yarns because bulky fibers may jam the sewing machine. This is the only time I recommend a very light blocking before stitching so that the edges are as flat as possible. Basting is especially important for machine-joined seams, so pin and baste first, then sew. Set your machine to the longest stitch, or if you have an electronic machine, set the stitch for knits. Sew the parts together in the same order as for hand sewing—shoulders, sleeves, underarms, and sides. After all these parts have been assembled, add any trims. Remove the basting stitches carefully to avoid breaking the machine stitching, then lightly steam the seams on the wrong side. Let the garment rest until it's completely dry. Turn it to the right side and check the seams again. Sometimes another light steaming on the right side may be necessary.

The method I prefer for connecting parts is the backstitch, with matching yarn, if possible. The backstitch forms a good solid, but flexible, seam that won't separate at stress points, such as shoulders and sleeve seams. The most expensive sweaters I've ever seen—like those knitted in France and Italy—are usually put together with a firm backstitch or they are machine stitched.

Match your sewing tension to the tension of the knitted stitches as much as possible. If the sewing stitches are too tight, the seam might pop, and that could be embarrassing. If they're too loose, the seam will not be stable. This requires a bit of practice. After you've done it a few times, you'll be able to discern the difference.

Use a blunt-point tapestry needle for this job. This type of needle is available in several sizes suitable for various thicknesses of yarn. They're inexpensive, so be on the safe side and keep several handy. Be sure they're blunt-pointed needles. A sharp point will split the yarn, which in turn will weaken the seam.

If the garment yarn is too bulky or nubby, making it difficult to thread the yarn through the tapestry needle, find a blending yarn in a lighter weight which is compatible with the main yarn. Use wool with wool, cotton with cotton, linen with linen, and so on.

A neckband to be attached after the garment is completed may be worked in a couple of ways. One way is to place, then pin, the band on top of the neck edge and carefully backstitch or overcast both edges of the band to the neck edge with very small stitches. Or you can attach the neck band to the garment with slipstitch crochet.

Patch pockets to be sewn onto the surface of a garment should first be positioned, then pinned and basted in place. To help you position the pockets, measure the distance toward the center of the body, and from the hem up, with a ruler. Use straight pins to indicate the top, bottom, and width of the pocket, then pin the pocket within that space. Knitted material is not rigid, so be especially careful. Your eyes can deceive you. After the pockets have been basted, lay the garment on a flat surface and stand away from it. Do the pockets seem even to you? If not, now's the time to make necessary adjustments, before taking up needle and yarn.

No matter how carefully all the seams have been put together, it may be necessary to firm up the back of a neckline or stabilize a shoulder seam. Seam binding, hand stitched across these areas, is usually all that's necessary. If the seam binding has not been preshrunk, dip it in hot water for a minute or two and let it dry thoroughly. This is something I've conditioned myself to do automatically. Cut a section of binding about an inch longer than the seam. Lay the binding on top of the seam with about 1/2 inch extra length at either end. Pin it to the seam, tucking in the extra binding at each end. With cotton sewing thread, tack the binding to the seam. The binding should be attached *after* the sweater has been blocked.

Use a strip of press-on fusible lining (available at fabric stores) to stabilize or ease in a neckline, pocket hems, or anything else that might need some support. Cut a strip long enough to cover the naughty area, then follow the directions for pressing the strip to the fabric. It will last through many launderings and is easily replaced.

The duplicate stitch (Chapter 8) is a super way to cover up a not-so-perfect seam. Worked in matching yarn, it will also stabilize the seam of a garment knitted with thick yarn. In a contrasting color, it can provide decorative detail.

There may be an occasion when an invisible seam is required, such as when attaching turned-back sweater cuffs or sewing up the sides of a turtleneck collar that's been knitted in two pieces. Since these areas are not considered stress points, the invisible seam is ideal. This is worked much like grafting (also called kitchener stitch), in that the seaming yarn follows the path of the knit stitches. When it's done correctly, it will be completely invisible from the right side of the garment.

To butt-join the sides of two pieces invisibly, thread your blunt-point tapestry needle with matching yarn. Pin together the two edges to be sewn, right side out, with T-pins placed crosswise over the edges. Starting from the bottom, pass the needle under the horizontal thread between the last two stitches of the right-hand piece and across and under the first two stitches on the opposite side. Work like this from one side to the other adjusting the edges, if necessary, until the seam is completed. Anchor the last stitch on the inside of the garment. This type of seaming is invisible as long as the thread is worked between the same two edge stitches. If hand sewing isn't one of your strong points, practice a few times before attempting this type of seam on your garment.

Edge finishes

You can finish a sweater with a knitted bias band sewn around the edge. The bias trim may be knitted or cut on the bias from woven material. To knit a band, cast on the number of stitches necessary for the intended width of the binding. For the first row, increase one in the first stitch, knit across to the last 2 stitches, knit 2 together. For row 2, purl across (for stockinette stitch) or knit across (for garter stitch). Repeat these two rows until the band is the correct length. To attach the band, pin one edge of it to the edge of the garment, right sides together, and backstitch the two edges together. Turn the band to the inside and carefully slipstitch in place. Be sure to watch your tension.

For a woven bias strip, cut strips of compatible fabric at least 1 inch wide on the bias, then stitch them together at a 45-degree angle so that the strips form one long, continuous piece. This requires some careful cutting and stitching, but you'll end up with an unusual finish to your sweater. The woven bias binding is attached *after* the sweater has been blocked.

Reverse single crochet produces a strong, firm seam or edge finish which I frequently prefer over regular single crochet. Do the single crochet in the usual manner, except work from *left to right* instead of from right to left. You'll have to shift your mental gears because almost every technique of crocheting or knitting requires that you work from right to left. The reverse stitch gives a more durable seam than conventional single crochet, and it is just as easily removed when necessary. It's a handsome exposed seam on the right side when worked in a contrasting color. Finish off a neckline or work a single row around the hem of a garment. Jackie edged her bateau neckline (page 25) with this stitch.

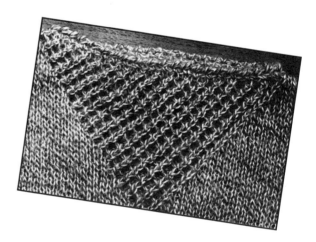

Detail of Jackie's eyelet yoke insert with reverse single crochet trim. The entire outfit is shown on page 25.

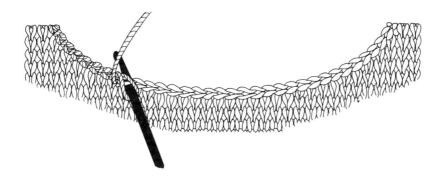

Reverse crochet trim is worked from left to right and can be done in a contrasting color for an interesting effect.

Loose ends

What do you do with all those loose ends? It depends where they are. If there are short ends in the body of your work from where a new yarn is connected, leave short tails and just let them hang free. Because the connection is already solidly knitted, weaving in isn't necessary. Those ends won't unravel. Besides, nobody but you will know they're there. This is completely opposite from what I have always recommended in the past, but there's a good reason. When I wove ends in, eventually some of them would begin to peek through to the right side and I was always poking them back into the material. But I do still advise working in any loose ends that may result from stitching seams.

Borders

Ribbed borders on cardigans appear to be a problem for many knitters. They have trouble sewing the border to the body of the garment so that the result has a smooth, professional look. Picking up stitches isn't always such a good solution, either, because the edge stitches may be too loose for a neat finish. I've found a simple way to pick up and knit the band at the same time. It works like magic. With a circular needle, in a size you'd normally use for the band (at least a size or two smaller than that for the body), starting at the right front (the left side facing you), pick up every "knot" edge

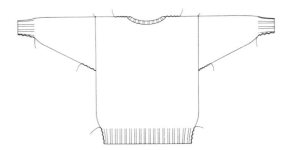

Loose ends can be left to hang free on the inside of the garment.

stitch up the left side, around the neck, and down the other side. Then on the same needle, cast on the number of additional stitches required for the border. For example, you may need to cast on 10 additional stitches. With a straight needle the same size as the circular:

Row 1: Purl 1, knit 1 across 9 stitches, knit 2 together, turn.
Row 2: Purl 1, knit 1 across 10 stitches, turn.

Repeat these two rows until there are 10 stitches remaining and you've worked up and all around the edge of the sweater. Bind off.

Each time you knit two stitches together, you'll be knitting one stitch from the new stitches and one stitch from the picked-up stitches on the circular needle, thus knitting and joining the band to the sweater each time. If buttonholes are to be included, knit them as you would ordinarily, evenly spaced. The band is a vertical rib that holds its shape beautifully, and all seaming is eliminated. The band may be made from plain garter stitch if you wish.

The same method may also be used to make a double band. Cast on twice the number of additional stitches necessary for the finished width of the band, plus one more for a slipped stitch which forms the fold back line in the middle. When planning a double band, if buttonholes are to be included, be sure to make a buttonhole on each side of the center slipped stitch. Use the same method for a neckline border, to edge sleeves, or for a band at the hem of a sweater. To place a band at the hem of a pullover, start at one side seam and work back around to that point. In this case, there will be a short sewn seam at one side.

Durable, attractive finishing demands care and a little patience. But it's not too hard. If your seams aren't perfect right away, don't be discouraged, you'll improve with experience.

Chapter 10
MAKING IT FIT

Would you throw out or give away a garment that cost a bundle because you no longer felt it was wearable? Wouldn't you at least consider the possibility of altering the garment? I certainly would. With the outrageous cost of quality clothes these days, few of us can afford to toss out an expensive garment. You'd be amazed how many people tell me about the handknits they no longer wear because their figures have changed or the knits are outdated, so they discard them or bury them in the back of the closet. It never occurred to them that those ill-fitting or outdated sweaters and skirts could be resurrected and made to fit and look like new again. These stories make me cringe. Yes, I know, the thought of unraveling stitches is repugnant, but with the cost of quality yarns today, can you honestly afford to literally throw money away?

At one of my workshops in Hawaii, a teenager was bemoaning the fact that by the time she'd finished her sweater—her very first—her body measurements had changed and she couldn't wear the sweater. She'd worked long and hard to do a good job, and she was so upset that she was ready to give up knitting and toss the whole thing in the trash. I showed her how to resurrect the sweater with some fairly easy alteration techniques that even a beginning knitter can handle. Actually, in her case, it was a matter of adding a couple of inches to the width and length of the body and sleeves. It wasn't necessary to unravel. Luckily, she still had some of the original yarn. But even if she hadn't, she would still have been able to achieve successful results with a contrasting yarn—perhaps making the sweater more interesting than the original design. In the process, this young woman collected a few more tricks to add to her knitting repertoire and renewed her enthusiasm in the craft. This young person's concerns set off a whole series of questions and answers about altering knits. Everyone in the workshop learned something useful that day. The rest of this chapter offers some suggestions that may be of help to you when you need to alter your knits.

Gussets

Gussets are a simple solution for a sweater that may require added width in the sleeves or in the body. Several types work for me—the long strip starting from the sleeve cuff all the way up the sleeve and down the side seam to the sweater hem; the small diamond-shaped insert for ease at the

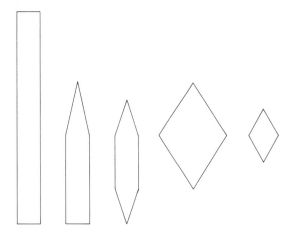

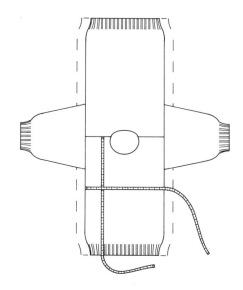

Several types of gussets can be used effectively to alter sleeves and side seams.

underarm; or the exaggerated diamond which will convert a conventional sleeve into a dolman. The gussets may be knitted from the same or contrasting yarn.

Before you start knitting away, undo the seams of your garment. (You need not undo all the seams when inserting the tiny diamond-shaped underarm gusset.) After the seams are opened, lay the pieces out on a flat surface. This will help you visualize where the added width is needed. Measure the width of the sweater and compare that measurement with your own measurement as it is now. If your body measurement is 2 inches larger than the sweater measurement, you will need to add at least 4 inches more to make the sweater fit comfortably. Each gusset should then measure 2 inches at its widest part. Now comes the creative part. If you have a ball or two of the original yarn, you're all right. If not, you must decide what other yarn will blend with the original. Do you have a record of the original stitch gauge and needle size you used?

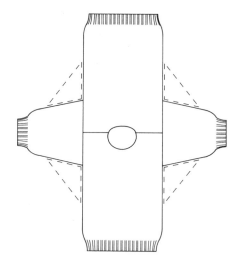

Top, undo the seams and measure the length and width of your sweater to determine how much altering needs to be done.
Bottom, add gussets at the underarm and side seams to provide the necessary additional width.

Can't remember? Knit up a couple of swatches in whatever yarn you'll be using, then cast on the correct number of stitches according to the gauge you select.

A long-strip gusset inserted between the front and back at the side seams is an effective way to increase the width of your sweater. For instance, if overall the sweater needs 3 inches of additional width, knit two strips about 1½ inches wide, plus two edge stitches for the seam allowance. Make the strips long enough to fit from the bottom of the sweater up the side to the underarm seams, tapering off gradually about an inch beyond the juncture of the sleeve and underarm connection. Should the sleeve need more width, instead of tapering off at the underarm, knit the strip long enough to continue to the cuff. For a sweater with ribbed hem and cuffs, start with the same length of ribbing at the hem, change to the stitch used for the body of the garment, and finish with cuff ribbing. Or you can start with the cuff and work in the other direction. Be sure to use the same size needles as used for the original sweater. To insert the gusset, turn the sweater to the wrong side and pin, baste, and sew the new pieces in place with backstitch. The new section will look as though it was meant to be there in the first place.

Try the elongated diamond-shaped gusset when additional width is needed at the bustline and possibly the sleeve as well. The gusset can be eased into the structure of the garment without distorting the original shape by tapering the new section gradually at each end. With matching or contrasting yarn, cast on two stitches and increase every second or third row until the gusset is the necessary width. Then work in reverse, decreasing instead of increasing. This gusset should be inserted so that one end falls just above the ribbed hem. Stitch it in place with a backstitch.

A tiny diamond-shaped gusset provides just a tad of ease to an armhole that binds. First decide how much new fabric is necessary for a comfortable fit. The widest part of the diamond should equal the number of inches necessary. Cast on two stitches, increase one stitch at the beginning and end of *every* row until the gusset is the correct width. Then decrease every row until two stitches remain. Bind off. Fold the gusset in half crosswise to find the centerfold. Open up the seams 2 or 3 inches on either side of the armhole and a couple of inches down from the top of the side seam and the top

A small diamond-shaped gusset can be inserted at the junction of the underarm and side seams for a more comfortable fit.

of the sleeve seam. Turn the sweater to the wrong side and pin, lining up the centerfold of the gusset with the juncture of the sleeve and underarm seams; then sew the gusset in place.

You can convert an old-fashioned tight sleeve into the newer dolman sleeve with a dolman-shaped gusset. This is my favorite sleeve design because it allows such freedom of movement. It will also immediately update your garment. Sometimes I've knitted this gusset with the same yarn as the original; other times I've used a complementary color with a completely different pattern stitch. For this type of gusset you should think BIG! Start with two stitches and *increase* at the beginning and end of every other row until the gusset is as wide as you desire, then immediately *decrease* every other row until two stitches remain. Bind off. This gusset should be inserted with the bottom point starting 2 or 3 inches above the top of the ribbed hem, and ending just above the cuff ribbing. If your sweater has a turned-back hem rather than ribbing, insert the gusset beginning a few inches above the top of the hem. Baste the dolman gusset before the final sewing to make sure it's properly placed.

Gussets may also be inserted when a sweater has been knitted with circular needles with no side seams. Turn the sweater to the wrong side and mark the place where a side seam might be. If the sleeves have a seam, use that seam as your guide. Run a basting thread in a contrasting color down the side of the sweater extending from the sleeve. On the sewing machine, stitch a line, using the longest stitch, down each side of the basting thread. Do this on both sides of the garment. As an extra precaution, I like to make double rows of

stitching. Hold your breath, and with very sharp scissors, cut between the machine-stitched lines along the basting. Don't be afraid, the double stitching will prevent the knitted stitches from unraveling. Before you attack the sweater, practice this on a piece of scrap knitting to see how it works. Knit the new pieces as already described. To insert the gusset, fold the two cut edges to the inside, just beyond the machine-stitching, then pin, baste, and sew in the usual manner. New sweater!

Altering skirts

Altering a handknitted skirt is actually easier than altering a skirt made from woven material—providing the skirt was originally knitted in panels from top to bottom, then sewn together (see Chapter 5).

To make the skirt larger, knit additional skinny panels and sew these new panels between the original panels. Let's look at an example in which your skirt consists of four equal panels and additional inches are needed from the waistline down to the hipline. You will knit two additional panels. Based on your new measurements and your stitch gauge, cast on the required number of stitches to start each panel at the waist. Then increase gradually, matching the original increases at the seams. Work down until the new panels are the same length as the skirt, work a turning row and hem if the original skirt has one, and bind off. Separate the old seams and pin, baste, and stitch the new panels between the original seams. You'll end up with a six-panel skirt—four large panels and two skinny ones. You'll still be able to switch the skirt around, but now you have even more possibilities because the new panels may work front to back or side to side. You may add as many new panels as you please, but for balance, add in multiples of two.

Lengthening and shortening

Occasionally some additional length is all that's necessary to resurrect a sweater or skirt destined for the scrap heap. If the sweater has ribbing, remove the old ribbing and knit the additional length you need. Your new stitches will be going in the opposite direction from the original ones, but this will hardly be noticeable. Or pick up stitches along the cast-on edge of the original ribbing.

To remove the old ribbing, remove the side seam stitching first to a point at least three rows above the top of the ribbed section. With your scissors, snip a loop at the outer edge of the material on both sides of the original seam and opposite each other. With a small knitting needle, or blunt-pointed tapestry needle, work out each stitch along the row until you reach the opposite edge. Slide the exposed loops back on your needle, making sure they are not twisted. The front thread of the loop should be slanting to the right. Undo the stitches of the second piece in the same way. Knit as many new inches as necessary, rework the ribbing, and bind off in pattern.

It is possible to pick up new stitches right along the cast-on edge and knit the necessary number of new inches, but be aware that you'll be a stitch off, so there will be a definite line. The new stitch will fall just a hair off-center of the original knit stitch. This could be an opportunity to introduce stripes of another color or two so the difference will be unnoticeable. Prevent disaster

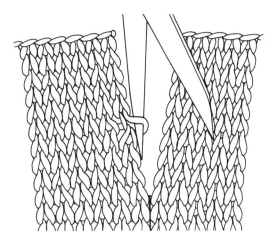

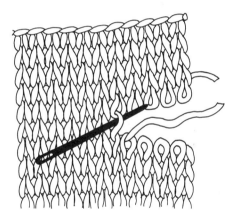

To remove old ribbing, separate the side seam, and snip a loop on each edge. With a needle, work out each stitch along the row.

before you plunge ahead and cut—practice on a sample first.

Here's how to lengthen or shorten a garment knitted from the top down all in one piece on circular needles. Mark the place a couple of rows above where you intend to make the alteration, and slip a stitch holder through two or three stitches. This will anchor those stitches and prevent them from unraveling. Lay the sweater on a flat surface and locate the line where a side seam would be in a seamed garment. Place a T-pin vertically at the place you intend to start unraveling; this is your traffic sign. Snip the horizontal thread between two stitches and work out the connecting thread as described earlier. Pull the cut end of the yarn through each stitch along the row until you return to the spot marked with the pin. As the stitches are being released, a long strand of yarn will accumulate. When it becomes too long and unwieldy, snip off a length 3 or 4 inches away from the material and continue on. After all the stitches have been exposed, carefully place them back on a circular needle, taking care not to twist them. If you should drop a loop, don't attempt to pick it up until all the stitches have been retrieved. Then, as you knit around to that spot, work it back onto the needle.

With luck, you'll have enough new yarn for the new inches. If not, unravel the cut-off material, wind it into a skein, and either steam the crinkles out with your steam iron or rinse it in lukewarm water, dry it thoroughly, and rewind it into a ball. Yarn from a previously knitted sweater will leave unsightly bumps in the new material if the crinkles are not removed before reknitting them. You should have no trouble with

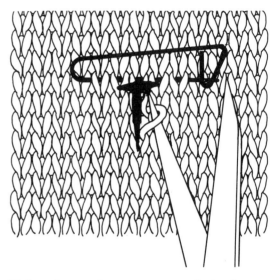

To lengthen or shorten a garment knitted on circular needles, slip several stitches on a stitch holder to prevent unraveling. Place a T-pin as a marker, snip a horizontal thread, and pull the cut end through each stitch on the row. Put the exposed stitches on a circular needle.

wool yarn, but man-made yarn may present a problem because once it's knitted, the bumps are often permanent. Try light steam on a sample without pressing down on the yarn. If the bumps straighten out, fine. If it's a lost cause, use new yarn.

Need to add a few inches in length? Undo the hem, separate the seams, and take out the bound-off row. Place the stitches back on the needles and work as many inches as needed, increasing if necessary to carry out the line of the skirt. Should there be a turning row at the hemline, you should unravel back to one row above the turn and then reknit.

Shortening or lengthening sleeves may also be done without unraveling the whole sleeve. To lengthen a sleeve, snip an edge stitch a couple of rows above the cuff, undo the stitches, place the released stitches from the main part of the sleeve back on the needle, and knit down the necessary number of additional inches above the cuff. Count your stitches. There probably will be more stitches than required for the cuff. On the next row, decrease those extra stitches evenly across the row, then begin the ribbing. Work in ribbing for the required number of inches, and bind off in pattern.

You may also add inches at the top of the sleeve. Remove the stitching around the armhole and a couple of inches along the sleeve seam. Undo the bound-off row, put the stitches back on the needle, and work the number of inches required. Bind off and reattach the sleeve to the body of the sweater.

To shorten a sleeve, decide on the new length, snip the edge stitch, release the stitches as described, and reknit the ribbing. Of course, you can also shorten the sleeve from the top as well. Remove the armhole

stitching and the bound-off row, unravel back to the desired length, bind off, and reattach the sleeve. Or snip the edge stitch, remove the excess material, put the stitches back on the needles, and bind off.

Stretching and fraying

When ribbed cuffs and hems stretch out of shape, get out the elastic thread and weave three or four parallel rows through the back loops of the stitches on the inside of the cuff. I'm not sure I could survive without elastic thread. I automatically weave it in as soon as the garment is completed, so stretched out ribbing is never a problem for me. It's the easy way out, but it works. Elastic thread can also be a solution for a stretched out neckline. If that doesn't work, remove the border or collar, and with a smaller needle, reknit a new one.

Don't you hate it when the sleeves wear out at the elbows when the rest of the sweater is still in good shape? Of course you can always sew a patch over the worn-out spot, or you might like to try this method on your next sweater. When knitting the sleeves, double the strands of yarn for about 4 inches at the elbow. Finish the rest of the sleeve with a single strand. From the right side of the garment the extra thickness will never show, but it does help to prevent fraying—at least for a while.

Any alterations require time and effort, but if they will rejuvenate a garment that is unwearable as is, don't you think it's worth it?

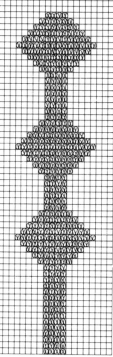

This white camisole, a companion to the slip-over on page 123, looks smashing under a tailored jacket for evening wear. The pattern was worked in reverse stockinette stitch on a stockinette background. The scalloped edges were made by knitting a row of openwork stitch and folding the fabric under along the yarn-overs.

Chapter 11
WITH LOVE AND DEVOTION

If you've loved it enough to spend time carefully selecting the yarn, creating a design, and finally knitting it, love your handknit enough to take good care of it.

Almost any yarn may be hand washed—with care. There are some exceptions, including suede and leather. First, read the instructions on the yarn label. If there are none, as with many weaving yarns, be sure to ask when you buy the yarn what laundering method is recommended.

Before you wash, draw an outline of the garment on a large piece of paper. If you don't have paper large enough, tape several pieces together. Add a few capfuls of pure liquid soap (absolutely no harsh detergents!) to a bowl of lukewarm or cool water, and swish the soap around a bit to work up a few bubbles. Gently lower the garment into the sudsy water. Lift it up and down a few times, squeezing to remove the soil. *No wringing!* Change the water several times until you're sure all the soap is rinsed out. Press the sweater against the side of the bowl to remove as much water as possible, carefully place it on a large towel, roll it up, and let it rest for a while. Have a cup of coffee, read a book, or knit on your new project while the towel absorbs more moisture. An hour should be plenty of time.

Lay the paper outline on top of a clean, dry towel, then place the sweater on the outline, move it around to fit the outline, flatten it with your fingers at the shoulder, side, and underarm seams until it looks as smooth as possible. Let it dry away from heat or sun. In most cases, no further blocking or pressing is necessary. If you aren't satisfied with the seams, lightly steam them with your iron—but don't press!

If you have one of those dryer racks made from screening, use it, although mine never seems large enough for any of my sweaters. It also doesn't fit across the bathtub as it's supposed to. You can make your own screen dryer in any size that's convenient for your purposes. Simply buy a piece of coated, rust-proof screening at the hardware store and fasten it to a window frame. The screen dryer allows air to circulate all around the garment for more efficient drying.

A mohair sweater may need some fluffing up after it's washed and dried. If you have a nylon hairbrush with large bristles, lightly brush it over the surface of the garment. Try not to pull at the stitches. Placing the sweater in a *cool* dryer for a *couple of minutes* after it's been air dried will also help fluff up the fibers.

So many different types of yarns are being combined that I have become concerned about dry cleaning processes. After hearing some real horror stories about ruined expensive handknits which had combinations of unusual fibers, such as fur, wool, leather, suede, and silk, I visited or telephoned several cleaning establishments here in Seattle and around the country to ask how they handle these garments. My research disclosed that many cleaners, in order to protect themselves, are requiring that the customer sign a waiver absolving the cleaning shop of all responsibility. I'm not saying you shouldn't knit with these types of materials—just be aware of the hazards before you make a final decision. Hand washing is still my first recommendation rather than dry cleaning because so often the odor of the cleaning solvent may remain.

Some leathers and suedes may be washed, but I haven't had much luck. I find that wiping smooth leather with a damp rag is acceptable. My suede sweater needs only a light going over with a fine emery board occasionally. Many cleaners specialize in cleaning leathers and suedes. It's expensive, but you're much wiser to let a professional handle it.

To help rid your knits of odors such as cologne, perfume, or mothballs, a few minutes in the dryer set to "no heat," with a dryer sheet, will often remove much of the odor without harming the garment. Add a couple of dry towels to cushion the action of the dryer.

Another question I'm repeatedly asked is, "What is the best way to store knits?" Ideally, they should be folded flat and stacked on a shelf or in a drawer. If you're fortunate enough to have generous shelf

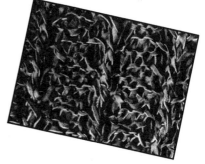

This sweater made from strips of suede can be cleaned up by using an emery board to brush away soiled spots.

space, slide your knits into an old pillow case or cover them with a piece of muslin to protect them, and store them on a shelf. We're not all blessed with enough closet space to indulge ourselves. It's a luxury I've secretly promised myself when I become rich—a whole room designed for storing only my handknits. Meanwhile, I've had to compromise and use lots of ingenuity.

Although you are constantly being cautioned *never* (there's that nasty word again) to hang your knits on hangers, there is a method that works for me, without any apparent damage to the yarn or shape of the garment. Gather up three or four plain wire hangers with those slim cardboard tubes. Tie or tape the hanger necks together, wrap a piece of fabric around all the tubes, and tape it down. Stuff the sleeves of your sweater with tissue, fold the sweater over the tube, and hang it in your closet. You can stack a couple of knits on the same hanger without bruising them and it saves closet space, too.

In some climates, bugs are a real problem. My friends in Hawaii suggested making a "bouquet garni" (a little bag made from a double layer of cheese cloth filled with whole cloves or bay leaves) and tucking it between garments. This may or may not ward off those pesky moths, but it's worth a try. Of course, there might be an odor of cloves or bay leaves—depending on whether you'd rather smell like a baked ham or a dill pickle. Whatever, it's better than smelling like mothballs or settling for moth holes.

And here's a valuable tip an ex-Navy friend told me about. When traveling, to save space and avoid wrinkles, lay a piece of tissue on top of your knit, roll the garment around the tissue, and tuck it in your suitcase. When you arrive at your destination, simply give the knit a shake and it will be wrinkle-free and ready to wear!

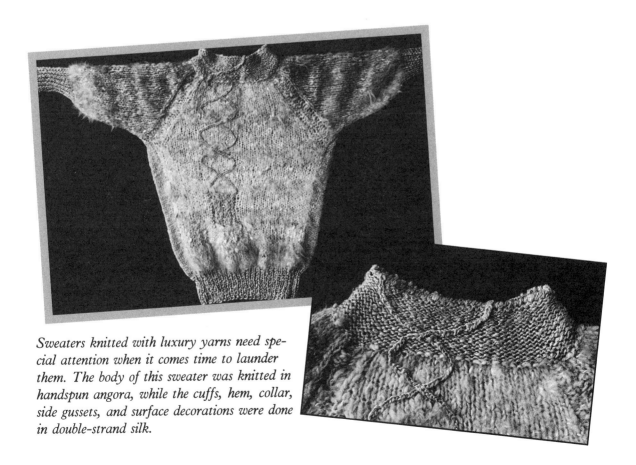

Sweaters knitted with luxury yarns need special attention when it comes time to launder them. The body of this sweater was knitted in handspun angora, while the cuffs, hem, collar, side gussets, and surface decorations were done in double-strand silk.

The horizontal ribbed bands on the sweater cuffs and hem, as well as the neck band, were worked in brioche stitch (see page 53). I ran a buttonhole placket down one side of the skirt for a tailored look. The skirt may also be worn with the Flanged Vest or the Greek Key Pullover.

Chapter 12
A COLLECTION OF DESIGNS

The sweaters in this section will give you some idea of the possibilities for creating one-of-a-kind designs using simple shapes and the basic principles presented earlier in this book. For some, I've given the basic information for you to apply to your own sweaters; for others, I've given more detailed instructions to show how the pieces were actually made. Stitch gauge and needle sizes are indicated only to show what I used to achieve an easy-fitting woman's medium size. I've noted yarn types, but not specific brand names. The idea is to offer you many possibilities, which you may execute to reflect your personal taste, measurements, proportions, and sense of style.

Study in Blue

This ensemble, made from a soft, luscious, hand-dyed wool, allows mix-and-match possibilities. Three different sweater tops pair with one basic skirt. A diagonal-knit pullover with horizontal ribbed bands uses the same yarn as the skirt for a coordinated, dressier look; a turnabout pullover with Greek Key motif uses solid blue for one side of the design, and a coordinating variegated yarn for the other; and a loose, sporty vest with stuffed shoulder flanges features wool and an angora-wool blend knitted together.

Diagonal Sweater Blouse

The tricky bias lines of this sweater are flattering to many figures, and easier to knit than you might think. Basically, you begin by knitting two triangles, which form the bottom two corners of the back. These are joined with a vertical band of four stitches in plain stockinette stitch, and then the back is worked in one piece to the top, with increases and decreases in each row creating the diagonal effect. If you follow my line-by-line instructions below, you'll find that a gauge of 5 stitches per inch will result in a woman's medium size. The ribbed pattern consists of 10 rows of stockinette stitch (knit 1 row, purl 1 row), with 6 rows of reverse stockinette (alternate knit and purl rows as for stockinette, but knit on the wrong side and purl on the right side).

Back: Cast on 2 stitches. Purl back. In stockinette stitch, increase 1 stitch at the beginning and end of every knit row 9 times (20 stitches). Begin pattern: in reverse stockinette stitch, work 6 rows followed by 10 rows of plain stockinette. At the same time, continue increases every *right side* row, until there are 42 stitches.

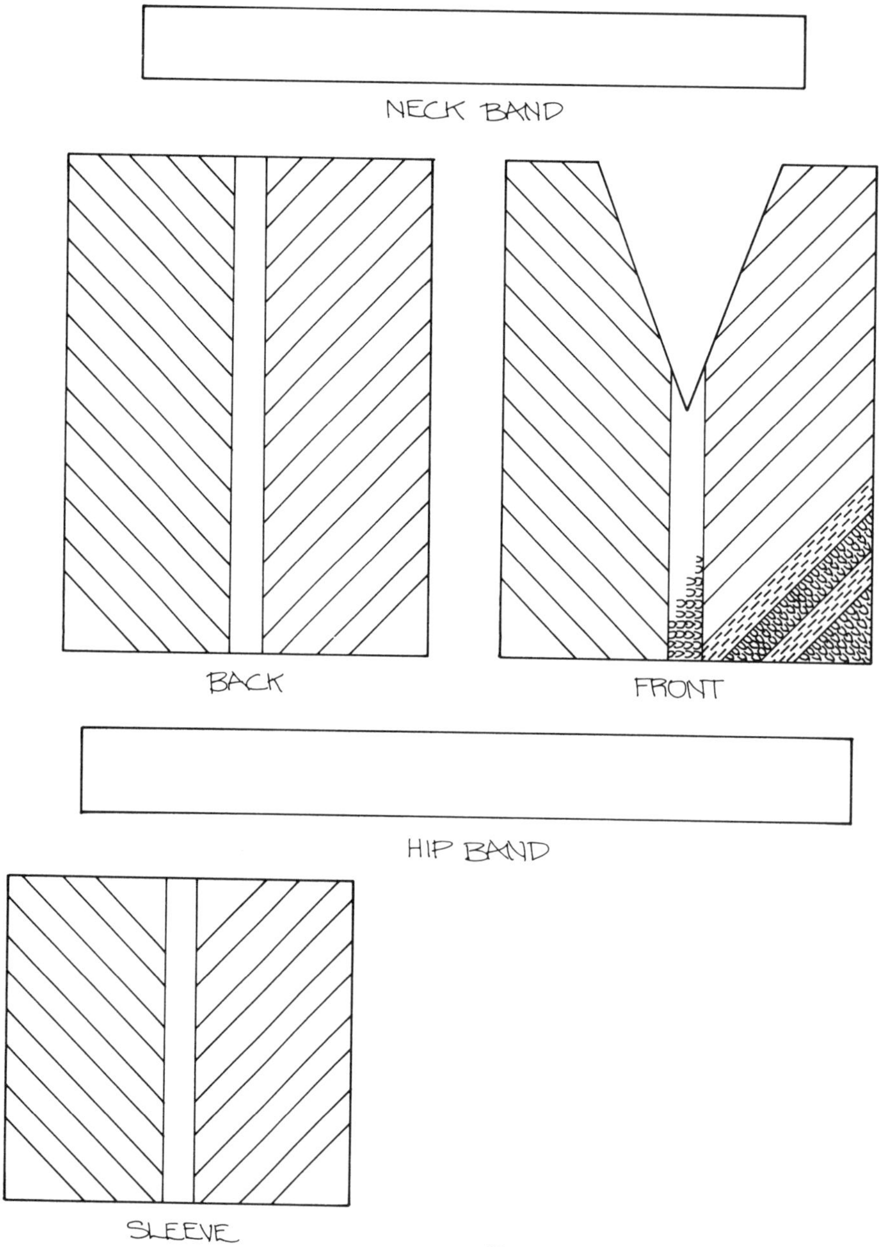

104

NECK BAND

BACK

FRONT

HIP BAND

SLEEVE

SLEEVE BAND

Pattern pieces for the Diagonal Sweater Blouse. The diagonal stripes were created by alternating stockinette stitch and reverse stockinette stitch.

Set this triangle aside.

With another ball of yarn, make a second piece to match the first.

To connect the two pieces, work across the first piece in pattern, cast on 4 stitches, and with the same yarn, work across the second piece (dropping the ball from which it is knitted). Work the next row (maintaining pattern), always working the center 4 stitches in stockinette.

On the next row, increase 1 stitch at the beginning of the row, work across to center, decrease 1 stitch in the last stitch before the 4 center stitches, place marker, knit 4, place marker, decrease 1 stitch, complete row, increase 1 in last stitch.

Continue working in this way, maintaining pattern, until the side edges measure 17 inches (or desired length). End on the wrong side. For a bias bind-off, bind off 2 stitches at the beginning of *every* row until 8 stitches remain. Bind off these 8 stitches.

Front: Work the same as the back. When the piece measures 10 inches, or desired length to neck opening, begin the V-neck as follows.

Work across to 4 center stitches, keeping pattern. Knit 2. Tie on a separate ball of yarn, knit 2. Complete row. Maintaining pattern, decrease 1 stitch at each side of the neck edge every 4th row until neckline measures about 5½ inches. On the next right side row, begin bias bind-off: bind off 2 stitches at the beginning of each side edge, still continuing neck decreases, until all stitches are bound off.

Sleeves: (make 2) Cast on 2 stitches. Working in stockinette stitch, increase 1 stitch at the beginning and end of every right-side row 5 times (12 stitches). Work in same pattern as body (10 rows stockinette, 6 rows reverse stockinette), continuing increases every right-side row until there are 34 stitches. Make another piece to match.

To connect these two corners, work as described for the sweater back, casting on 4 stitches between parts. Work in diagonal pattern, and in addition, increase 1 stitch at the beginning and end of the right-side row every ¾ inch, until the sleeve measures 14½ inches (or desired length). Bind off 2 stitches at the beginning of *every* row until 8 stitches remain. Bind off remaining stitches.

Hip band: I worked this piece in brioche stitch (see page 53), using a needle three sizes smaller than I used for the body:

    Row 1: Knit.

    Row 2: Knit 1, knit 1 in stitch *below*.

    Repeat these two rows.

Cast on 16 stitches, or whatever even number you want the width of the band to be. Mine is about 3½ inches wide. Work in pattern until the band is 1 inch less than the measurement of the sweater bottom. Bind off in pattern.

Sleeve bands: These are worked the same as the hip band; I made mine about an inch narrower, casting on 12 stitches on the smaller needle size. Work the sleeve bands until they measure 2 inches less than the bottom of the sleeves. Bind off in pattern.

Neck band: With smaller needle, cast on 12 stitches or any even number to give the width you want. Work in brioche stitch until the band fits around the neckline. Bind off in pattern.

Sewing up: With right sides of body together, backstitch shoulder seams, matching up pattern stripes. Fold sleeves in half, place pin at fold, pin center of sleeve to shoulder seam with right sides together, and carefully backstitch in place. Stitch hip and sleeve bands in place, easing in bottom circumferences to fit. Stitch neck band to neckline.

Flanged Vest

I used the same blue yarn as for the Diagonal Sweater Blouse, along with a complementary angora blend yarn. Knitting with these two yarns together required larger needles (size 11 and size 10½), and resulted in a gauge of only 3 stitches per inch.

The body of the sweater is knitted in stockinette stitch (knit 1 row, purl 1 row), the neck border in garter stitch (knit every row), and the ribbing in sand stitch (see page 52):

Row 1: Knit.

Row 2: Knit 1, purl 1.

This vest is knitted all in one piece—no shoulder seams! With smaller needles, cast on 52 stitches, and work in sand stitch for 3 inches. Change to larger needles.

Row 1: Knit.

Row 2: Knit 4, purl across to last 4 stitches, knit 4.

Continue in this way, but increase 1 stitch *after* the first 4 stitches, and *before* the last 4 stitches, on the right side rows, every 1½ inches, 3 times (58 stitches). Work even until the piece measures 20 inches (or desired length) before garter stitch neckline border. Knit 4 rows of garter stitch all the way across.

On the next row, in pattern, work 22 stitches, bind off the next 14 stitches for neck, work remaining 22 stitches.

On the next row (wrong side), knit 4, purl 14, knit 4; tie on another ball of yarn, knit 4, purl 14, knit 4. On the next row (right side), knit 22 for each side. Continue working both sides in this pattern until neck measures about 10 inches, ending on the wrong side.

On the next row, work across in pattern to neck edge, cast on 14 stitches for center neckline, and complete row with the same ball of yarn (dropping second ball). Knit 4 rows of garter stitch. Then work down the back, reversing instructions for front, and decreasing instead of increasing.

Flanges: Fold body in half at shoulder and mark center with a pin. Fold back the 4 border stitches to the right side, and with smaller needles, pick up 8 stitches on either side of marker along the inside edge of the garter stitch border. Purl back.

At the end of the row, pick up 5 more stitches. Turn, knit across row, pick up 5 stitches at end of row. Continue working in stockinette, picking up an additional 5 stitches at each end until there are 66 stitches. Bind off. Make another flange on the opposite side.

Sewing up: Roll the flanges to the inside around soft, fat upholsterer's cording, and slipstitch in place. Lap one front over the back and pin to the depth of the ribbing. Overcast ribbing on right side, turn and slipstitch on wrong side. Sew the other side in the same way.

This one-piece vest features shoulder flanges stuffed with upholsterer's cording to give it a sporty look.

This striking Greek Key Pullover can be worn with either side as the front. Note the covered button at the hem for surface decoration.

Greek Key Pullover

This boldly-patterned drop-shoulder pullover uses the blue skirt yarn for one color, and the same variegated angora-wool blend as the vest for the other. As you can see from the detail photograph, the pattern is created by changing colors partway across each row. The point at which the color change is made controls the movement of the pattern. One sleeve is worked in blue with a two-stitch stripe of the variegated yarn running right up the middle; the other sleeve is worked with the yarns reversed. Ribbings are worked in twisted rib, a firm knit 1, purl 1 ribbing in which you knit in the *back* of each knit stitch. The cowl collar is described on page 80. It may be worn front to back with the design reversed.

Blue Skirt

The skirt for this ensemble is worked from the top down in three pieces, as shown in the diagram. It's more tailored than most knitted skirts, with a button placket running down one side and a kick pleat and mitered hem. After all my raving about eliminating buttonholes, I decided to include them in this design. You can omit them, sewing the opening together and adding some interesting buttons evenly spaced down the length of the band. Or you can eliminate the band altogether.

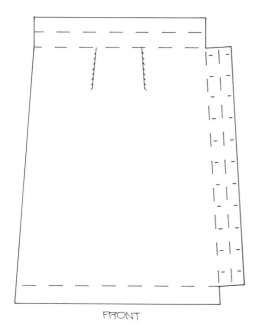

FRONT

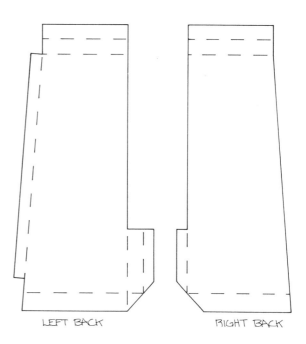

LEFT BACK   RIGHT BACK

Pattern for blue side-buttoned skirt with back pleat.

Black and White Smocked Sweater

The black yarn in this dolman-sleeved sweater blouse is a sport-weight smooth wool, and the exaggerated yoke is a white wool-mohair blend. The generous sleeves have an added-on insert running their full length from ribbing to shoulder, and the neckline is finished with a simple rolled collar. Using size 7 and size 9 needles, my gauge was 5 stitches per inch. I started from the top of the yoke and worked to the V, but you can work from the bottom up if that seems easier. Whichever way you work, be consistent so that the back and front are the same. (Actually there isn't any back and front—it's a turnabout.) Leave the underarm seams for last.

Back: With smaller needles, cast on 108 stitches. Work in knit 1, purl 1 ribbing for about 4 inches. Change to larger needles, and work in stockinette stitch, increasing 1 stitch at the beginning and end of a knit row every inch, 3 times (114 stitches). On the next right-side row, knit 57 stitches, tie on another ball of yarn, and knit to the end of the row. Working both sides at the same time, decrease 1 stitch each side of the yoke edge (center) every knit row until work measures about 19 inches, or until all the stitches have been used up. Fasten off.

Front: Work the same as the back.

Sleeves: (make 2) With smaller needles, cast on 58 stitches and work in ribbing for 3 inches, ending on purl side. Change to larger needles, knit 20 stitches, bind off center 18 stitches, tie on another ball of yarn, and knit remaining stitches. Working both sides at the same time, increase at the beginning of row on first piece, and end of row on second piece, every 4th row until work measures 21 inches, or desired length. Bind off.

Sleeve inserts: With smaller needles, cast on 88 stitches. Work even in stockinette stitch for 3 inches. Bind off.

Yoke: (make 2) With mohair and larger needles, cast on 159 stitches. Work in pattern:

Row 1 (right side): Purl 4, knit 1, across row, ending with purl 4.

Row 2: Knit 4, purl 1, across row, ending with knit 4.

Work even in pattern for 1½ inches, ending on wrong side. On next row, maintaining pattern, start decreasing 1 stitch every other row until all stitches have been used up. Fasten off.

Sewing up: With right sides together, backstitch yoke pieces to body pieces. Stitch shoulder seams, leaving an opening large enough for your head (about 8 inches wide). Be especially careful to match up ribs. Backstitch insert bands to sleeves, across bound-off stitches of cuffs, up one side and down the other. Stitch sleeves to armholes. Work smocking as described on pages 68 and 69. Sew underarm and side seams.

With a circular needle in smaller size, and right side facing you, pick up stitches around the neckline and work in stockinette stitch for 2 or 3 inches. Bind off loosely.

Some Variations: If you'd rather eliminate the dolman sleeve, start with the ribbed cuff and immediately above the cuff, add as many stitches as you desire, then knit straight up to the appropriate length, eliminating the center section. Make a version of this from cotton, linen, or rayon—it doesn't have to be wool, but keep in mind that these other yarns have less flexibility.

This black wool sweater has a
smocked white mohair yoke. The
smocking ribs were stitched with
the black wool of the sweater.

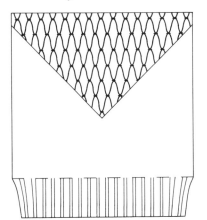

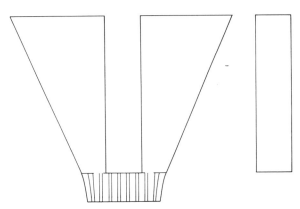

Summer Cooler

This sweater, made from gray, glossy cotton with white linen accent stripes, is a variation on the dolman shape of the Black and White Smocked Sweater and the pattern technique of the Greek Key Pullover. Other combinations of yarns would be effective, too—see what you can do with the basic ideas.

As you can see from the diagrams, this sweater is knitted in only two pieces, with the sleeves incorporated into the front and back. This is accomplished by starting at the ribbing, knitting with gradual increases for about 5 inches above the ribbing, and then increasing 3 stitches at the beginning of *every* row until the sleeves are the desired length. The piece is worked even for about

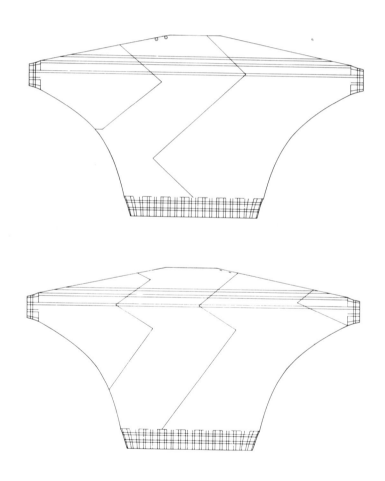

Design for both sides of Summer Cooler.

Dolman sleeves and braided trim at the neck accent this reversible pullover made from shiny gray cotton with white linen stripes.

6 inches, and then bound off 3 stitches at the beginning of each row until only the neckline is left. The neckline stitches are bound off all at once.

The diagonal texture patterning results from working part of a row in stockinette and the rest of the row in reverse stockinette. The point at which the stitch pattern changes shifts by one stitch in each row. It's easy—you don't have to worry about changing yarns.

In sewing up this sweater, I left one shoulder seam open for a couple of inches. The neckline is finished with a row of single crochet around the neck and shoulder opening, with 2 chain loops for buttons on the shoulder. The decorative braid around the neck is made of 3 crocheted chains— 2 gray, 1 white, each about 1½ times as long as the opening. I braided the chains together and stitched them to the neckline with matching thread.

Rainbow Sweater

This easy sweater is made from odds and ends of baby fingering yarn in yellow, turquoise, pink, and white. It would be smashing in several bright colors with black, too. My gauge with size 6 needles was 6 stitches per inch. If you haven't tried side-to-side knitting, this shape would be good to start with. This sweater is knitted all in one piece; there are no shoulder seams.

Body and sleeves: Beginning at one sleeve edge and with any color, cast on 120 stitches. Knit even in stockinette stitch for ½ inch, and make a turning row by purling a row on the right side. Continue in stockinette stitch, changing color about every 2 inches, until work measures about 7 inches. Change color and work another ¾ inch. Cast on 54 stitches at the beginnings of the next 2 rows (228 stitches). Work even in stockinette stitch for 8 more inches, continuing to change colors as desired.

Divide for neck: Work halfway across (114 stitches), slip remaining stitches on a holder. Work even on 114 stitches, changing color every 2 inches or so, until neck opening measures about 8 or 9 inches. Place the

The Rainbow Sweater was knitted from side to side instead of from bottom to top. This is an easy way to achieve vertical stripes in your designs.

stitches you've been working on a holder. Work stitches from the first holder to match those already knitted. When this piece measures the same as the first one, work across 114 stitches, and across the 114 stitches from the holder. Continue to work even in stripes (even or uneven widths, as you please). When this side of the body measures the same as the first one, bind off 54 stitches at the beginnings of the next 2 rows (120 stitches). Work even until sleeve measures the same as the first sleeve, including turning row and hem. Bind off.

Ribbed hem: (front and back are the same) With right side facing, pick up 110 stitches evenly spaced along bottom edge in any color with smaller needles. Work knit 1, purl 1 ribbing for 3 or 4 inches. Work ribbing on other side in the same way.

Neckband: With any color and smaller needles, right side facing, pick up 64 stitches across one side of neck opening. Work knit 1, purl 1 ribbing for about ¾ inch, decreasing 1 stitch each side of every other row twice. Work a turning row by knitting across on right side. Continue ribbing for about ½ inch. Bind off in pattern. Make a neckband on the other side in the same way.

Sewing up: Sew up short ends of neck bands, turn to inside, and slipstitch loosely. Sew side and sleeve seams in one long seam. Turn sleeve hems to wrong side and slipstitch.

If you're short on yarn, as I was, fool around with the stripes. They don't all have to be exactly the same width. Ribbing may replace the sleeve hems, too.

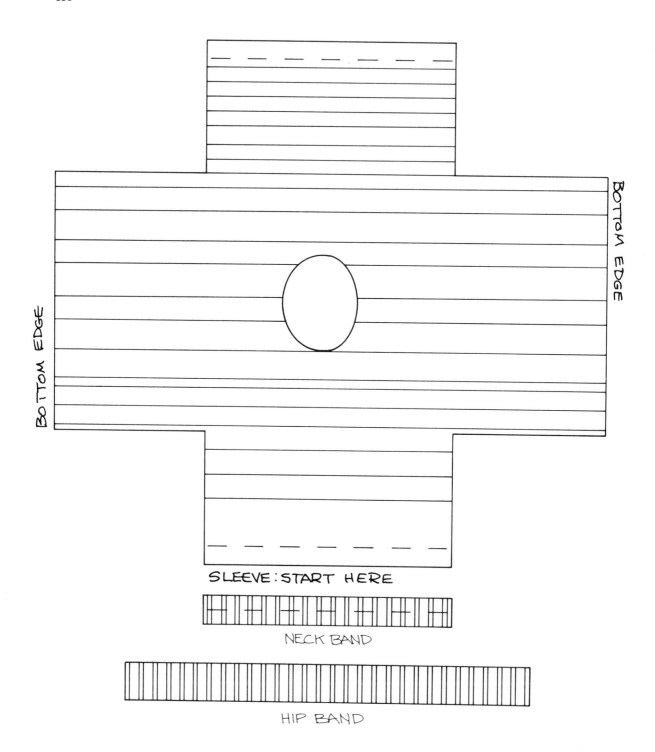

BOTTOM EDGE

BOTTOM EDGE

SLEEVE: START HERE

NECK BAND

HIP BAND

*Left, design for Rainbow Sweater. The
horizontal lines indicate where colors were
changed. Above, back of Rainbow Sweater.
The sleeve hems may be ribbed for a different
look.*

Bouquet Sweater

The simplest sweater shape takes on new dimensions when it's a canvas for colorful freeform designs. This sweater is made from four rectangles; its slight shape comes from a ribbed hem held in with elastic thread. The sweater is knitted throughout with two strands of a shimmery rayon blend yarn with a slight texture. The flowers are a loopy multicolored rayon lace yarn in shades of light and dark blue, rose, celery green, and aubergine. The flower motifs extend into the ribbings—a fun touch, and easy to do. If you'd prefer a boxy look, eliminate the ribbings and work straight from the cast-on row and then finish the bottom with a row or two of single crochet.

This one-size-fits-all design knits up quickly on size 11 needles (size 9 for the ribbings) at a gauge of 3½ stitches per inch. The shoulders are especially wide. If they seem too generous for your figure, you can simply thread a double strand of yarn through the shoulder seams on the inside and gather them up as much as you like.

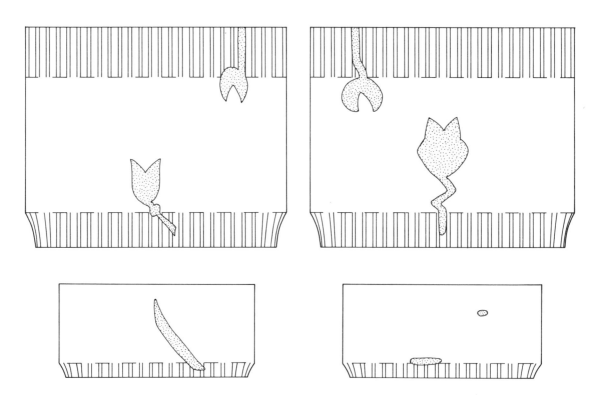

Design for bodice, above, and sleeves, below. The multicolored flowers allow this sweater to be coordinated with a variety of skirts and slacks.

Sweater Abstracts

It's fun to knit a sweater side to side, because it provides an easy way to include abstract shapes without having to carry a bunch of bobbins. This sweater is one example of the possibilities of this trick. The yarn is cotton with a slubbed texture, and the multicolored inserts are a glossy, smooth rayon yarn. Every once in a while I inserted a bit of the open fan stitch used in the orange mohair on page 55 just for the fun of it. They look like stretched stitches, but they are there on purpose. If you don't like this effect, forget it.

Because of all the texture and pattern in this sweater, I ruled a pattern stitch out as excess baggage. So the body is simple stockinette. However, I used seed stitch for the cuffs, and added a cable detail on the hip and neckline bands—and they worked out fine.

On size 10 needles (size 9 for the ribbing), my gauge was 4 stitches per inch.

Body and sleeves: With smaller needles, cast on 56 stitches. Work even in seed stitch:

Row 1: Knit 1, purl 1 across.

Row 2: Purl 1, knit 1 across. You will be knitting the purl stitches and purling the knit stitches.

Work rows and partial rows with the multicolored rayon, as shown in the diagram. When work measures 2 inches, change to larger needles. Working in stockinette stitch, increase 1 stitch at the beginning and end of every knit row until there are 110 stitches, then cast on 3 stitches every 4th row, twice. Cast on 38 stitches all at once at beginning and end of the next 2 rows. Work even until piece

This sweater features a double row of cable around the hip band and a single row of cable at the neckline. The bold, abstract pattern was created by knitting from side to side.

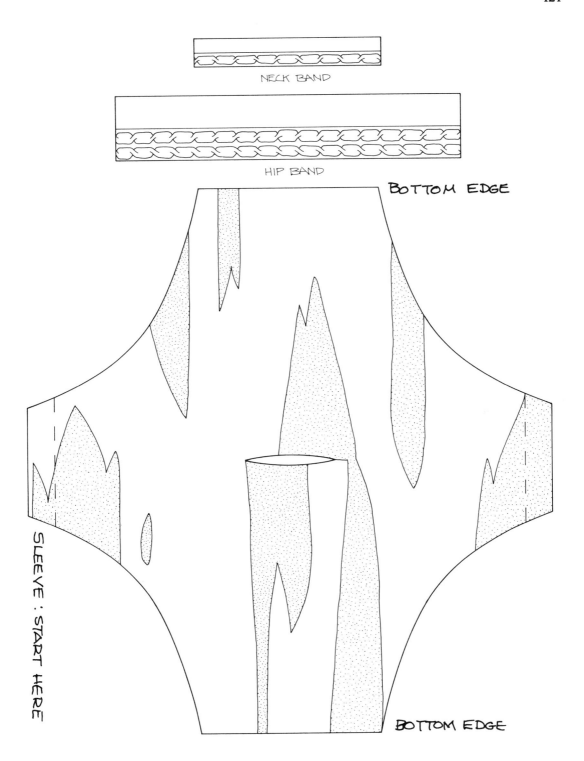

NECK BAND

HIP BAND

BOTTOM EDGE

SLEEVE : START HERE

BOTTOM EDGE

measures about 22 inches. Divide work in half for beginning of neckline, and tie on another ball of yarn. Continue in pattern, working on both sides of the neckline, for about 9 inches.

Now work across all the stitches with one ball of yarn, dropping the second ball as you come to it. Work even until this half of the sweater measures the same as the first half, reversing all shaping (decreasing and binding off instead of adding stitches). Bind off.

Cable neckband: With smaller needles, cast on 16 stitches.

Row 1: Knit 6, *purl 1, slip next 4 stitches to a holder and hold in back, knit 4, knit 4 from holder*, purl 1.

Rows 2, 4, and 6: Knit 1, purl 8, knit 1, purl 6.

Rows 3 and 5: Knit 6, purl 1, knit 8, purl 1.

Repeat these 6 rows until the band is long enough to fit easily around the neckline.

Cable hipband: With smaller needles, cast on 36 stitches. Knit the first 14 stitches, then work double cables as described on page 59. Work until band fits bottom of sweater.

Sewing up: With right sides together, pin, baste, and sew side and sleeve seams. Sew neckband to neck opening by folding back the stockinette facing and stitching it to the inside of the neck opening. With right sides together, pin, baste, and sew cable edge of hipband to bottom edge of sweater. Fold facing to the inside and slipstitch in place loosely. Lightly steam seams, being careful not to flatten cable.

White Slipover

This little slipover is knitted in a lightweight wool yarn that would be ideal to wear under a summer suit, with a full, swingy cotton skirt, or with sleek black satin evening pants. Stylized floral motifs are worked in reverse stockinette for subtle design interest. This is one of the few sweaters in this book with shaped sleeve caps; this feature helps it work under other garments without too much bulk. Add shoulder pads to the barely puffed sleeves to broaden the shoulder line, if you wish. Using size 6 needles for the body (size 5 for hems), my gauge was 6 stitches per inch.

Front: With smaller needles, cast on 96 stitches and work knit 1, purl 1 twisted rib (knitting into the *back* of all knit stitches) for about 2½ inches. Change to larger needles and knit across, increasing 1 stitch at the beginning and end of the row. Purl back. Position flower motifs as you please (or omit them); stitch markers will help you keep your place in this tone-on-tone design.

Working in stockinette (except for flowers), increase 1 stitch each side every 1½ inches 6 more times (100 stitches). Work even until piece measures 12 inches (or desired length to armholes). Bind off 2 stitches at the beginning of the next 2 rows, then decrease 1 stitch at the beginning and end of every other row 8 times. Knit even until armhole measures 9 inches, or desired length, ending on a purl row.

Neckline: Knit 27, bind off center 24 stitches, tie on another ball of yarn, knit 27. Working both sides at the same time, purl back. On next row, and next

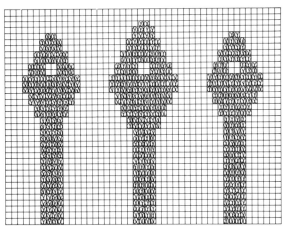

2 *knit* rows, decrease 1 stitch at each neck edge. Work 3 inches even, and bind off.

Back: Work the same as the front.

Sleeves: (make 2) With larger needles, cast on 66 stitches. Work in stockinette stitch for 4 rows, ending with a purl row. On the next row, knit 1, *yarn-over (yo), knit 2 together*, repeat across the row. Purl back, knitting the yarn-overs. Knit 4 inches even. Bind off 2 stitches at the beginning of the next 2 rows. Decrease 1 stitch at the beginning and end of every knit row 8 times. Work even until sleeve measures same as armhole opening. Bind off.

Sewing up: With right sides together, pin, baste, and sew shoulder seams. Sew sleeves to armhole, easing the fullness in at the top of the sleeves. Sew sleeve and side seams.

With a circular needle in the smaller size, and starting at one shoulder, pick up 164 stitches evenly spaced around the neck edge. Knit 1 row, purl 1 row. On the next row, knit 1, *yo, knit 2 together*. Purl 1 row, knit 1 row. Bind off loosely. Fold the neckline trim at the yarn-over row to the wrong side, and slipstitch loosely. Sew sleeve hems the same way. Lightly steam the seams.

The picot or eyelet edge at neck and sleeves offers a bit of froth to this simple sweater blouse.

The floral motif at right was knitted in reverse stockinette stitch on a stockinette background. See page 98 for another example of this subtle design technique.

Mohair Yummie

This sweater is the same basic shape as Sweater Abstracts, but the design has been simplified to make the most of the soft, luscious 100% mohair. Colors are the softest shades of peach, variegated pink and white, and ecru; the vertical stripes blend, rather than divide, the garment, so it would be suitable for almost any figure type. The neckline is finished with several inches of plain stockinette, which rolls back on itself for a neat finish. Applied cuffs are plain knit 1, purl 1 ribbing. This sweater is also reversible.

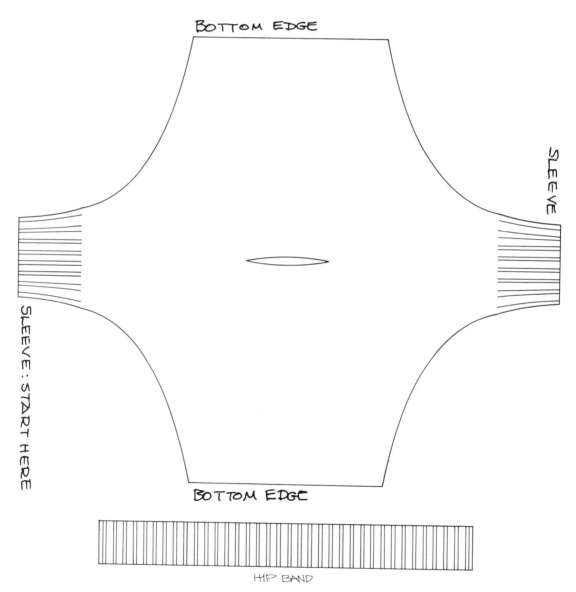

This luxurious, reversible mohair sweater was knitted from side to side. The subtle stripes, knitted with a silk and rayon yarn, add textural interest without being too bold. When the sweater is worn front to back, the stripes run over the other shoulder.

Sweater Twins

What could be more classic and adaptable than a twin set? I designed this pair for a very lightweight yarn, but you could use almost anything if you watch your stitch gauge. My yarn is dove gray, and works up to a gauge of 6½ stitches per inch on size 5 needles. The simple designs feature a sleeveless crew neck undersweater and an open V-neck buttonless cardigan. Progressively narrower horizontal bands of ribbing add textural interest, but you could use almost any stitch, either in bands, or as an allover pattern.

Sleeveless Sweater

Back: With size 4 needles, cast on 126 stitches. Work in knit 2, purl 2 ribbing for 4 inches. Change to size 5 needles, work 10 rows of stockinette stitch, 8 rows of ribbing, 10 rows of stockinette, 6 rows of ribbing. Work even in stockinette stitch for 6 more inches (or the desired length to the underarm). At the beginning of the next 2 rows, bind off 3 stitches, then decrease 1 stitch at each armhole edge every knit row 6 more times. Work even until armholes measure 8½ inches (or desired length). Bind off.

Front: Work the same as the back until 2½ inches from the final length. Bind off center 24 stitches. Tie on another ball of yarn and, working both sides at the same time, bind off 3 stitches at each side of the neck 3 times. Work even until armhole is the same length as the back. Bind off.

Neckband: With circular needle in smaller size, cast on 120 stitches. Work in knit 2,

purl 2 ribbing for 2 inches. Bind off loosely in pattern.

Sewing up: With right sides facing, backstitch shoulder seams. Pin, baste, and sew side seams. Turn armhole edges about ½ inch to the inside and slipstitch in place. Pin, baste, and sew one edge of neck band to neck opening. Fold to inside and slipstitch other edge to inside.

Cardigan

Back: With smaller needle, cast on 130 stitches. Work ribbing sequence the same as for the pullover, then work even in stockinette stitch until piece measures 16 inches or desired length. Work in ribbing for 6 more inches. Bind off.

Left front: With smaller needles, cast on 84 stitches. Work 62 stitches in knit 2, purl 2 ribbing. Place marker, purl 1, knit 10, place marker, slip 1, knit 10. This establishes the front band and facing.

On the next row, purl 21, knit 1, work in ribbing as established. Work in ribbing, and knit front band between markers, to match back, until work measures 12½ inches. Shape V-neck by decreasing 1 stitch before first marker every 4th row, and at the same time, work last 6 inches in ribbing. Continue decreasing at neck edge until piece is the same length as the back.

On the next knit row, bind off all stitches up to the first marker. Work the remaining 22 stitches as established, until this band will fit around half of the back of the neck. Bind off.

Right front: Work to match left front, reversing all shaping.

Sweater Twins can be worn separately or as a set. The cardigan features ribbed pockets at the hem and set-in sleeves. The sleeveless shell has a crew neck and narrow bands of ribbing for texture.

Pockets: (make 2) With smaller needles, cast on 32 stitches and work in ribbing until pocket is the same depth as the sweater ribbing. Bind off in ribbing.

Sleeves: (make 2) With smaller needles, cast on 52 stitches and work in knit 1, purl 1 ribbing for 2½ inches. Change to larger needles and work in stockinette stitch, increasing 20 stitches evenly spaced across row. Increase 1 stitch at beginning and end of next 8 knit rows. Work even until sleeve measures 20 inches, or desired length. Bind off.

Sewing up: With right sides facing, sew shoulder seams, matching ribbing. Sew sleeves in place, positioning sleeve center to shoulder seam. Sew sleeve and side seams. Sew short ends of neckbands together. Fold front facing to inside at the ridge formed by slipped stitches, stitch bottom of facing, then stitch facing to inside. Sew bottom edge of back neck band to neck edge. Fold band to inside and sew. Pin pockets to sweater, matching ribbing, and overcast around 3 edges.

Smoke Ring

Some of the sweaters in this book are knitted from wonderfully luxurious, one-of-a-kind yarns. Silks, cashmeres, alpacas, angoras—when you have yarns like these, you want to give them your best design shot to create a unique and wonderful garment.

Sometimes, though, you might want to try just a bit of an elegant yarn to get the feel of it before tackling—and blowing your budget on—a large quantity. This smoke ring scarf is a perfect quick project for such an occasion. It's a nice use for leftover yarns, too. Here's how:

Cast on enough stitches, according to your stitch gauge, to measure about 18 inches (this is the depth of the ring). Knit a bias strip by increasing 1 stitch in the first stitch, and knitting the last 2 stitches together, on every other row. Work bias in stockinette or the stitch of your choice, adding other colors if you wish, for about 22 inches. Bind off on the wrong side. Connect the two short ends (see page 87).

To convert the smoke ring to a hood, just add as many more inches of stitches to the width as you need to fit over your head. Nothing to it!

Stephanie's Back-To-School Duds

The sweaters we've looked at so far have been fashion-conscious grown-up styles. But some of the most enjoyable knitting I've done has been for my grandchildren. This hooded jacket, jumper skirt, and matching leg warmers are easily adapted for big kids, too. The jacket is completely reversible (turn it inside-out for a different color arrangement), and may be worn by a girl or boy. I've given instructions for it; you can easily adapt the skirt and leg warmer sketches to the size you need.

The colors are bright red and navy. I didn't have enough of one color for a complete ensemble, so I alternated the two; little kids like the kooky color arrangement. All the pieces are knitted mainly in stockinette, with no shaping—just rectangles sewn together.

The yarns are worsted-weight synthetics; my gauge was 4 stitches per inch on size 10 needles. Stephanie is about a size 4.

Back: With size 10 needles, cast on 50 stitches and work 2 rows in garter stitch. On next row, increase 1 stitch in every stitch across the row. Continue in stockinette stitch for 5 inches. End on a purl row. On the next row, knit 2 together across the row. Knit the next row. On the next row, knit, increasing 1 stitch in every stitch across the row. Work until piece measures the same as the previous section between increase and decrease rows. Make as many sections as you need for the necessary length. Bind off. Make another piece to match this one *in a different color.*

Fronts: (make 4 pieces—2 in one color, 2 in another) Cast on 25 stitches and knit as described for the back. Bind off.

Sleeves: With needles 2 sizes smaller (size 8) and one color, cast on 26 stitches and knit 2 or 3 inches in knit 1, purl 1 ribbing, adding stripes of contrasting color if desired. On the next row, change to larger needles, increase 16 stitches evenly spaced across the row, then work even until the sleeve is the desired length. Knit the second sleeve in the other color.

Sewing up: With right sides together, pin and sew one front to one side of back, leaving space for sleeves, matching up garter stitch divisions, and alternating colors. Sew the other front to the other side. Sew remaining three sections in the same way. Pin both back shoulders to front shoulders, then slipstitch crochet through all 4 pieces. Turn garment to right side, and pin all

pieces together down fronts, along bottom, and around neckline.

Hood: With smaller needle, right side facing you, pick up 40 stitches around neck through one layer, and work in ribbing for 1½ inches. Change to larger needle, and increase 20 stitches, evenly spaced. Work 10 inches in stockinette stitch. Bind off. Turn work to wrong side.

With smaller needles and other color, pick up the same number of stitches through the other layer. Work the lining of the hood the same way as the first layer. Bind off. With right sides together, fold bound-off edge of one hood in half, and backstitch edges. Do the same with the other side of hood.

Turn jacket right-side out. Pin edges together starting at lower right back, up sides, leaving sleeve opening, and along edge of hood. With crochet hook, work a row of single crochet around bottom, up sides, and around hood. Insert a double-sided zipper for front closing so that the jacket may be easily reversed.

Fold sleeves with right sides together, matching up ribbings, and slipstitch crochet the edges. Pin sleeves to armhole openings, matching sleeve seams to side seams. Single crochet to armholes.

Drawstring for hood: Make a braid from the two colors, tie strong knots at either end, then weave through the ribbed neckline.

To make the jacket longer, simply remove the side connections, pick up stitches along the bottom edge, and add new sections. The skirt can be lengthened in the same way. To add length to the jacket sleeves, remove them from the armholes, remove bound-off row, and knit up from there.

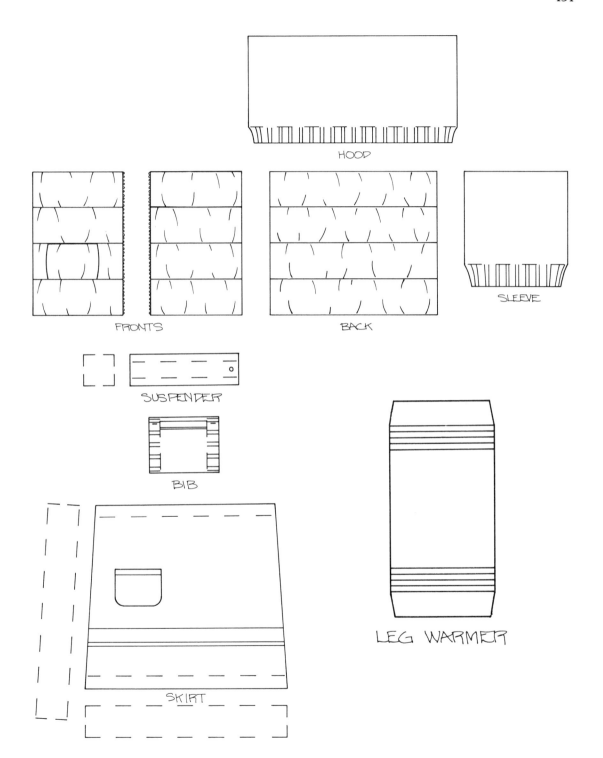

HOOD

FRONTS

BACK

SLEEVE

SUSPENDER

BIB

LEG WARMER

SKIRT

This sweater was made from bias strips of woven cotton plaid fabric. You need not be confined to conventional yarns once you understand the basic principles of designing and knitting.

Knitted from strips of woven cotton, this scoop-neck pullover has tiny cap sleeves and a matching skirt. It was knitted by Cynthia's daughter.

Chapter 13
IT AIN'T NECESSARILY SO.

So many absolutes were handed down to me when I first became acquainted with knitting—skirts must *always* be knitted with circular needles from the bottom to the top; seams must *always* be flat and woven together; the needles must *always* be held in a certain way; the parts should *always* be blocked before connecting them; and you should *never* add an extra stitch or you'll ruin the design. All those rules nearly turned me off from knitting forever. But I'm stubborn. It was like waving a red flag in front of a bull. I began to experiment and question, and vowed to eliminate those two nasty words—always and never—from my knitting vocabulary.

A whole new world of knitting opened up when the realization hit that the only restrictions were those I put on myself. I didn't need anyone's permission to experiment. So experiment I did. Frequently those experiments were the direct result of laziness or because I was in a hurry, but each time I learned something new. The worst that could happen would be some unraveling if things didn't turn out as expected. I could live with that—unraveling didn't bother me as long as the end result was wonderful.

Knits may be worked from bottom to top, from top to bottom, from side to side,

from corner to corner, or whatever other direction you invent—as long as it works. Once you begin to understand why and how things work, you'll have gained complete control of the needles and yarn. Are you just beginning to enjoy the craft? Then keep an open mind. Having worked with hundreds of knitters of every age, from rank beginners to the most highly skilled, I have found that those with the most developed technical skill and greatest speed are rarely the most successful. These knitters have the greatest difficulty unhooking themselves from rigid, preplanned structure. They are completely dependent on the commercial pattern designed by someone else—strictly by the book. They never question, and thus don't understand why things happen. They're missing most of the fun. Beginners will more easily accept a challenge. They haven't been exposed to all the "don'ts," so they are willing to try. These are the knitters who will be the most successful and satisfied.

I want to share a story with you. A young woman who had just learned to knit came to see me one day. We were in the midst of photographing garments for this book, and knitted stuff was spread all over the place. When Bonnie saw the melange of color and texture she could hardly keep her hands off. She was bursting with excitement.

She had just finished her very first sweater—and it fit! And no one had told her how—she learned by ripping and reknitting, with determination. Eagerly, she began to inspect all the garments, looking at shapes, inspecting the seams, and all the while asking questions nonstop. I hadn't seen such unbridled enthusiasm in a long while. We professionals can get pretty jaded, you know. "How do you know how to do all this?" she asked. So I proceeded to explain some of my thinking to her. What impressed her most, I think, was that the horizons were almost unlimited. As we chatted, Bonnie mentioned how she first became interested in yarn. She learned to spin while on a trip to New Zealand. Her husband said he couldn't understand why she wanted to spin yarn when she didn't know the first thing about knitting. This discussion occurred the day before her return to the United States, so time was precious. Being a determined person, she went to the nearest knitting shop and persuaded the owner to teach her how to knit. The owner thought it was strange that she didn't know the craft because everyone, from kindergarten on up, knows how to knit in that part of the world. After her brief introduction to knitting, Bonnie practiced on the plane all the way home, with everyone around offering advice.

This woman will be a super knitter because she isn't afraid to unravel when the results are less than satisfactory, and of even greater importance, she is willing to take a risk. As a novice with motivation, she's well on her way!

Lee, the youngest member of the knitting group, was also the most inexperienced and was somewhat hesitant about attempting to create her own design. But she was determined. She chose a lovely, high-quality wool in a medium blue to complement her bright blue eyes, fair skin, and light hair. Her jacket features little puffed sleeves (I think only the young can get away with these sleeves), with a cable front and neckline border. The neckline seemed to sag a bit, so after a light steaming, she stitched a length of cotton bias tape across the back of the neck. This held the neckline in place enough to solve that problem. Her enthusiasm was so high that she was already thinking about her next project. After listening to all of us discuss matching skirts, she, too, planned a skirt.

Lee's wool sweater was knitted in stockinette stitch with twisted rib cuffs and cable trim.

Carolyn knitted a matching cap to go with her crazy-striped pullover.

Carolyn was also cutting her teeth on individual design. She knitted a sweater and matching hat based on ideas recommended in one of my earlier books. The front and back are exactly the same, with all the stripes matching perfectly at the side seams. The sleeves match, as well. A similar plan of striping was carried out in the hat. She did say that next time, instead of increasing the width of the sleeves from cuff to shoulder, she would increase all at once above the cuff and knit the sleeves straight up. For her first attempt at original design, I think she did beautifully. The sweater is attractive, it fits, and she loves it. And that's what knitting is all about.

Bev, on the other hand, loves the challenge of complicated pattern stitches and is a stickler for precision. After much shopping around, she carefully chose a soft blue-green heather yarn for her outfit. In order to dress up a fairly simple shape, she combined "Angel Hair" (an iridescent, fine synthetic fiber) with the heather wool. The combination is smashing. Her skirt features six gores with some flair beginning just above the knee. She found out the hard way (by unraveling) that constricting armholes and sleeves no longer looked fashionable, nor were they comfortable. She ripped them out and redesigned them. She also used an interesting pattern stitch down the front and the sleeves to add vertical interest.

Final word

Knitting is an incredible craft. Just think of the fantastic, beautiful things that emerge from two little sticks and a ball of yarn. I'm not sloshily emotional about knitting, although I know many people who are. The enjoyment of creating an original design with beautiful yarn is enough for me. I like the way the material feels when I'm working with it and when I wear it. The sense of pride carries me along all through the process. It's a lovely feeling of accomplishment.

By now I hope I've encouraged you to try your wings and develop enough self-confidence to enjoy the freedom of choice available to you as a knitter. It is my wish that you appreciate the flexibility of the knitted fabric and are willing to make it work for you (not the other way around); that you can indulge your fantasies, but with intelligence; that you've decided to be willing to experiment and even make a few mistakes along the way; that you give yourself permission to do anything you please. And most important, realize that no matter what your level of skill, beginner or experienced, and no matter what your age, shape, or size, you can produce fashionable, comfortable, long-lasting knits—designed by YOU!

Appendix

Metric Conversion Chart

Yarn weights and measurements in other countries are usually computed using the metric system. To help you make comparisons, here is a conversion chart that gives *approximate* differences.

    1 ounce (oz.) = 28 grams (gm)
    3 1/2 ounces = 100 grams
    15 ounces   = 420 grams
    1 inch (in.) = 2.5 centimeters (cm)
    1 foot (ft.) = 30 centimeters
    39.4 inches   = 1 meter
    1 yard (yd.) = 90 centimeters

Needle sizes

American	Continental (mm)	British
00	2	14
0	2.25	13
1	2.5	12
2	2.75–3	11
3	3.25	10
4	3.5	9
5	3.75–4	8
6	4–4.5	7
7	4.5–5	6
8	5–5.5	5
9	5.5–6	4
10	6–6.5	3
10½	6.5–7	2
11	7–7.5	1
	8	0
13	8–8.5	00
15	8.5–9	000

Index